W9-CPE-641

Uncommon Cards

Stationery Made with Recycled Objects, Found Treasures, and a Little Imagination

Jeanne Williamson

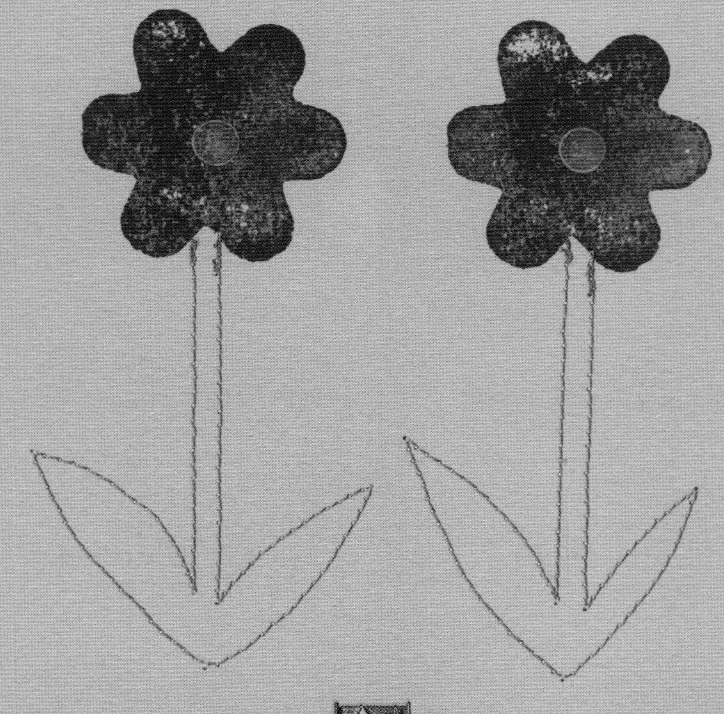

RUNNING PRESS
PHILADELPHIA • LONDON

© 2013 by Jeanne Williamson

Published by Running Press,
A Member of the Perseus Books Group

All rights reserved under the Pan-American and International Copyright Conventions

Printed in China

This book may not be reproduced in whole or in part, in any form or by any means, electronic or mechanical, including photocopying, recording, or by any information storage and retrieval system now known or hereafter invented, without written permission from the publisher.

Books published by Running Press are available at special discounts for bulk purchases in the United States by corporations, institutions, and other organizations. For more information, please contact the Special Markets Department at the Perseus Books Group, 2300 Chestnut Street, Suite 200, Philadelphia, PA 19103, or call (800) 810-4145, ext. 5000, or e-mail special.markets@perseusbooks.com.

ISBN 978-0-7624-4566-0
Library of Congress Control Number: 2012942464
E-book ISBN 978-0-7624-4927-9

9 8 7 6 5 4 3 2 1
Digit on the right indicates the number of this printing

Cover and interior design by Kristina Almquist Design
Illustrations by Kristina Almquist
Edited by Kristen Green Wiewora
Typography: Adobe Garamond, Trajan, and American Typewriter

Running Press Book Publishers
2300 Chestnut Street
Philadelphia, PA 19103-4371

Visit us on the web!
www.runningpress.com

A very special thank-you
to my husband and best friend,

Joshua Ostroff,

for being supportive of me, and my art,
for 30-plus years.

Contents

Acknowledgments

I am thankful to many professionals, family members, artists, and friends in my life for helping me to bring this book to you.

I am very grateful to everyone with whom I worked at Running Press for their help, expertise, and creativity in bringing this book to life, especially my editor Kristen Green Wiewora, project editor Annie Lenth, and designers Frances Soo Ping Chow, Bill Jones, and Ryan Hayes, and publisher Chris Navratil.

Thanks to my agent Sorche Fairbank, who worked very hard in making this book a reality, as well as my previous book *The Uncommon Quilter*; to Kristina Almquist, who I have known since my very first day of art school way back when, for creating wonderful illustrations and for designing this book; and to Joel Haskell, for his portrait photography and patience.

Many thanks go to my husband, Joshua Ostroff. This project would never have come to fruition without his love and support. I would also like to thank family members Jonah Ostroff, Rebecca Ferrell, and Elaine Ostroff for your love and support as well.

Thank you to many artists, Linda Levin, Catherine Carter, Laraine Armenti, Leslie Rogalski, Michael Rogalski, Catherine Evans, Merill Comeau, Margot Stage, Martha Wakefield, Wendy Young, Jane McKinnon Johnstone, Brenda Cirioni, Adria Arch, Anne Krinsky, Kathleen Volp, Christiane Corcelle, Dianna Vosburg, and Carol Schweigert, for your professional support, friendship, and encouragement in the many years I have known you.

I would also like to thank Carol Hildebrand for sharing ideas and materials, and Nancy Poorvu, Gladys Cohen, and Kathleen Mahoney for your kindness and support. If I have neglected to add anyone who has helped me, I thank you, too, and apologize for not mentioning your name!

Introduction

For as long as I can remember, I have been making my own cards, and the reasons vary.

When my husband and I were planning our wedding many, many years ago, we wanted our invitations, RSVPs, and thank-you notes to have a theme that wouldn't have translated through what was then offered through a commercial printer. Instead, I created a line drawing of the design of our wedding chuppah, a canopy Jewish couples stand under during their wedding ceremony, which I appliquéd with symbols of our wedding rings, a wineglass and napkin, hearts, and daisies, and had it printed on card stock. Then, my soon-to-be husband and I spent many hours hand coloring the cards with colored pencils. The end result was a unique set of cards that were made with love, and which cost very little.

When our son was born a number of years later, we naturally did the same thing for his baby announcement and thank-you cards, as by then we were very experienced at card coloring. My husband designed the text on his mid-1980s work computer, which was very pixilated compared to computers now; I pasted it, with glue, to a black-and-white line drawing I made of confetti and balloons; and we had it printed. While our son was napping, and we should have been, too, we bonded as new parents by coloring the cards, once again with colored pencils.

There have been other times when my husband and I have made cards together, but in recent years he's taken to making cards by drawing with markers on unusual sizes and shapes of scrap paper, and there's also the occasional computer-generated fake ransom note that kids love as birthday cards. I gradually transitioned to making one-of-a-kind paper cards on my own, using my sewing machine. I wanted to make cards that were unique, that had texture and were sewn, so I didn't have to be concerned about glue affecting the paper, or waiting for it to dry if I was in a rush when sending a card.

Sewing paper, instead of fabric, is not difficult, but it definitely has its pluses and minuses. One difference is that you can't pin pieces of the card elements to the card stock in advance: once you pin or sew a stitch, the hole is there forever. It does take a little planning to make a card, but the result is well worth it.

The most positive part about making cards is that the recipients know it was made especially for them, with love. I hope you'll enjoy it, too, and that this book will give you many ideas and a lot of inspiration.

—Jeanne Williamson

CHAPTER 1

Getting Started

This book is for the new or experienced sewer, for any type of creative artist who is looking to try something new, and for those who don't consider themselves artists but who like to play with materials.

When making greeting cards, it's fun to experiment with new ideas, techniques, and materials. That's why this book will show you how to make cards with unusual techniques, as well as uncommon or found materials.

Inside this book you'll find fifty-two projects divided into three categories: found objects, fabric and paper, and surface design. Each card project includes simple step-by-step instructions, which you can follow to produce the cards pictured in this book, but you can also use the projects as a jumping-off point for creating your own cards.

The purpose of this book is not to make perfectly crafted cards. Instead, it was written to share the fun and creativity in card making, and to offer you an opportunity to try something new, as well as something that is not offered in other books about making cards.

There are no rules to follow when making your own cards. If you are an experienced sewer, you may choose to turn under the edges of your fabric when appliquéing, or sew perfectly spaced stitches. However, when making a card, the length of your stitches is not important, as long as they are not so short that they rip through the paper. When working with pieces of fabric, you can leave the cut edges unfinished, and you may or may not want to use a simple zigzag stitch to keep the edges from fraying.

There are also instructions in this book about how to construct an envelope for a fully handmade look, which is especially useful if the cards you make are unusual sizes. As when making your own cards, there can be a lot of flexibility and fun in making an envelope. Because this book focuses on stitching cards, the instructions for making an envelope also include stitching and offer a completely different form of envelope construction than you may have considered.

This book uses appliqué techniques (sewing pieces of fabric to the card), but it also pushes the envelope by appliquéing unusual objects and recycled materials, such as several different types of paper, netting, ribbon, lace, rickrack, candy or cupcake wrappers, yarn, or pieces of shopping bags.

There are also a number of unconventional surface design techniques, such as hand stamping with fruits, vegetables, and rubber erasers or pencil erasers; making crayon rubbings; and hand coloring.

As you start making the cards in this book, feel free to improvise as you dream up designs of your own. Use my cards as inspiration for generating your own ideas.

SETTING UP YOUR WORKSPACE

Whether you have a dedicated workspace for your card making or you are making room at the kitchen or dining room table does not matter. What is important is that you have a clean work surface. Take a moment to clear some space from the table. Remove any food or beverages from the area so there are no unexpected spills on your materials.

TRYING NEW THINGS AND TAKING RISKS

As you make the cards, please keep in mind that sometimes you will make mistakes, or the card might not work out the way you expected it would. Making mistakes is a valuable learning experience. Sometimes making a mistake is unavoidable. Some of the materials might not be as easy to sew as you expected, the sewing machine may not appreciate sewing it, it might slip, or it might come out crooked. Problems or mistakes like these can lead to a new discovery and might lead to a more creative solution. I suggest that you don't throw your mistakes out. They can be useful for future reference, or the card stock might be a useful place to experiment before making another card.

You might want to create a card on your own, in addition to or instead of following the instructions in this book. Look for ideas online, in magazines and books, or at a craft or fabric store, or make time to visit a gallery or museum. Many artists keep a sketchbook or journal where they write or draw ideas and collect photos, magazine or newspaper clippings, or printouts from inspirational websites.

FINDING TIME TO CREATE

Sometimes it might be difficult to find the time to make a card for a certain person or occasion. Consider making a date with yourself to create. Or think about making a collection of cards ahead of time that you can access as you want or need to use them. Making them ahead of time might be especially useful for cards that can be used as sympathy cards, because that's most likely the time you might need a card when you least expect it or don't have time to make one.

BASIC MATERIALS

To make your own cards, there are a number of materials you will want to have on hand. Some projects may call for more specific materials, but overall, the basic supply list includes the following:

- Card stock—different colors and sizes
- Thread—colors that contrast and match the card stock, as well as black and white thread.
- Sewing machine or needles for hand sewing
- Scissors
- Ruler
- A sharp pencil

You don't need to buy all these materials brand new to get started. Many can be found around your home or office, at yard sales, in discount or secondhand stores, or via www.craigslist.com or www.ebay.com.

CARD STOCK

Cards can be made with many kinds of paper. That includes writing paper, printer paper, 3 x 5-inch (7.5 x 12.5 cm) cards, old wrapping paper, cut-up paper bags, and more. Although any of these papers can be used, cards are more commonly made with card stock.

Card stock comes in different weights that are heavier than paper but lighter than cardboard. It also comes in many different sizes, textures, and colors and can be purchased in packages or in individual sheets.

Some card stock is included in this book so you can get started right away. When you want more card stock, or if you would like different colors or sizes, you can purchase it at craft or office supply stores, as well as online.

Most, but not all, of the cards used as examples in this book were made with card stock from the Paper Source. I like the colors and the range of sizes available in its line of folded cards. Most of the cards I used measure 5 1/2 x 5 1/2 inches (14 x 14 cm) or 5 x 7 inches (12.5 x 18 cm), though the Paper Source does offer other sizes, too.

POSTCARDS

The blank postcards I used are 4 x 6-inch (10 x 15 cm) Strathmore postcards, which are available at some art stores and also online. The postcards are a somewhat heavier paper than the card stock.

In addition to buying blank postcards, feel free to also use thin cardboard (but not corrugated cardboard), 3 x 5 (7.5 x 12.5 cm) cards, and any other thick paper that's available to you.

When you decorate your own postcards, try to limit your sewing to the outer edges and the very center of the paper, so the stitching that goes through to the other side doesn't make it difficult to write, address, and stamp the postcard.

CARD COLOR

When choosing card stock, consider using both light and dark colors. Don't let concerns about writing a note on a dark color steer you away from dark card stock. There are two ways to write on the card: Use an opaque white or light-colored marker, or sew (or glue) a piece of white paper onto the dark paper.

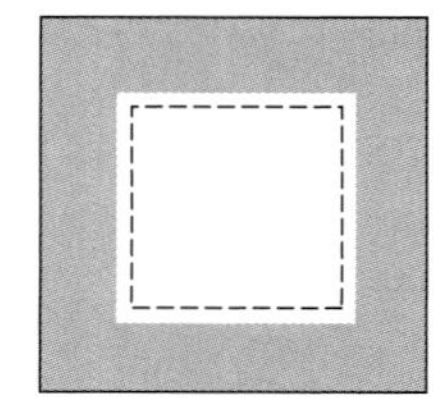

SEWING

If you are not a sewer, consider borrowing a sewing machine from a friend or neighbor before buying your own. If you don't have access to a sewing machine, or you can't afford one, or you prefer to work with your hands, you can hand stitch your cards. I prefer a sewing machine because my hands get stiff when hand sewing, and the results are fast.

Before using your sewing machine, make sure that you have enough thread on the spool and in the bobbin. Running out of thread while sewing can cause a surprise line of stitched holes with no thread.

When setting up your sewing machine, check your presser foot and look to see whether you have more than one kind. Most sewing machines come with one main style of presser foot, which will work just fine when stitching the various materials to create your cards. But if you are a quilter, or just so happen to have a walking foot for other reasons, that might help to keep both the top and bottom materials from slipping as you sew. So, if you have a walking foot, don't hesitate to use it.

Every time you start and end a stitched line on your card when using a sewing machine, be sure to anchor your stitch, by either going forward and backward for one or two stitches, or anchoring the stitches in any other way you're used to. If you are a sewer, you already know that you need to do this when making clothing or home goods. That is also true when sewing cards.

If you decide to hand sew your cards, they will have a beautiful look and feel all their own. Because cards are small, the amount of time and labor involved with hand sewing should be relatively quick. Most of the cards in this book can be hand sewn with no trouble.

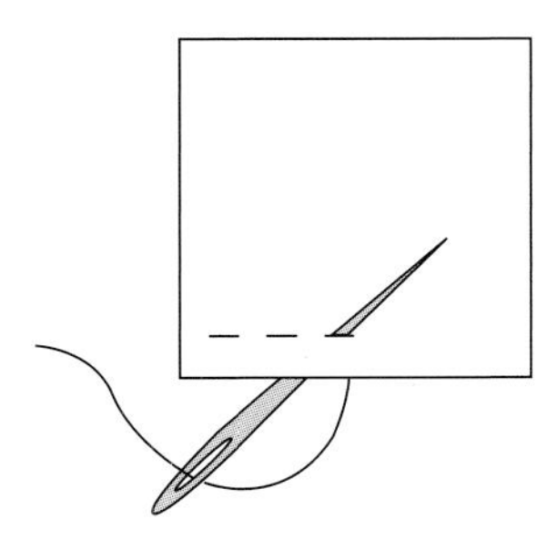

The instructions in this book can easily be adapted to sewing by hand. I suggest knotting the end of the thread as you start sewing a line, and when you finish, knot the end of the line before you cut the thread.

Whether sewing using a sewing machine or by hand, the stitch size should be of medium length. A line with very short stitches might rip through the paper. If you have extra card stock, I advise you to try sewing different stitch lengths so you can get a feel for sewing on paper, and to experiment with the different effects.

I also advise you to experiment with the size of the needle, whether sewing with a machine or by hand. I use a medium-size needle when working in either method. If the needle is too thin or small, it might not pierce the paper, or it might break. If it's too thick, it might make an unnecessarily wide hole that will interfere with the design, or it might rip the paper.

STITCHING PAPER

Once a hole is made in the paper, it's always there. Think before you sew. If you need help finding the center of the card, or help with getting everything straight on the page, be sure that you measure before you get to work.

THREAD

Many types of thread are available for sewing. For the projects in this book, I suggest that you use regular sewing thread, the same thread you would use when sewing clothing or many home goods.

You can try using thicker threads, but I encourage you to sew them on a scrap piece of card stock first, so you see how it looks on the paper and see whether you like the increased texture.

The colors of thread for the card front will vary with each of the card instructions. Sometimes it will match the card color, and other times it will create contrast. While thread colors will be suggested for each card, feel free to change the color as you like. You may want to use a different color than suggested for design reasons or because you might not have the suggested color.

Most of the card instructions will encourage you to try to match the color of bobbin thread with the card stock color. Using a similar or matching bobbin thread will help make the sewn lines inside of the card be less noticeable, and will also give the card a more professional look.

If you don't have a bobbin thread that matches the card color, or if you forget to change the bobbin thread to match it, all is not lost. One choice is to just let the thread color be what it is and not be concerned if it doesn't match. If you really want it to match, find a marker that closely matches the card color, and lightly color the bobbin thread with the marker. You might want to try this on a practice card before you do it on the actual card, so you know how the thread reacts to the marker, to decide whether you like the effect, and to see what happens if the marker slips off the thread onto the card stock.

Hand sewers may want to choose between the suggested thread and bobbin colors and decide which color would be a better choice. Typically, the suggested bobbin color is the same color as the card stock, and the thread for the front of the card is a different color. Either will work for your design. Basically, you will be choosing between a matching card color versus a contrasting color. If you have extra card stock and a few extra minutes, you could try making the card twice, trying both colors, to see which you prefer.

AN ALTERNATIVE TO SEWING

If you decide to use glue instead of sewing by machine or by hand, use small amounts of glue to attach items to the card as an alternative to the stated instructions. Consider experimenting with glue, on an extra piece of the kind of paper you will be using, before working on the actual card, just in case the paper starts to curl or get lumpy. If it does, try using a different kind of glue, not as much glue, or press it flat with something clean and heavy, such as a pile of books. To avoid getting any glue on your weighty object, I suggest placing a piece of waxed paper or aluminum foil between the card and the weight. The glue shouldn't stick to the foil or waxed paper, though that depends on what kind of glue you use.

Because stitching decorative lines won't be possible, try using a felt-tip pen or fine marker, with or without a ruler to draw the lines.

MEASUREMENTS AND MEASURING

The instructions in this book are flexible and are provided more as inspiration than as rigid directions.

When finding the center of the card front, you can find the center, or as close to center as possible, by eye, or you can choose to measure to find the exact center.

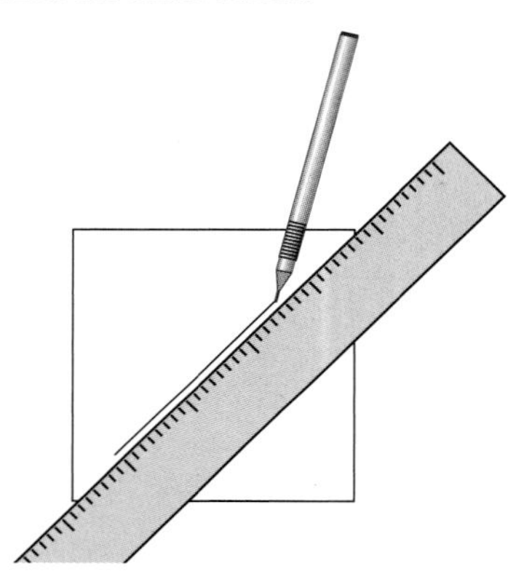

If you want to find the center by measuring, place a ruler from one corner to the corner at the one that is diagonally across the center of the card. Divide the measurement in half. Using a pencil, place a small, light dot at the center measurement.

If you don't feel confident about creating or spacing straight lines for your design or for sewing straight lines on the card front, there are simple ways to measure.

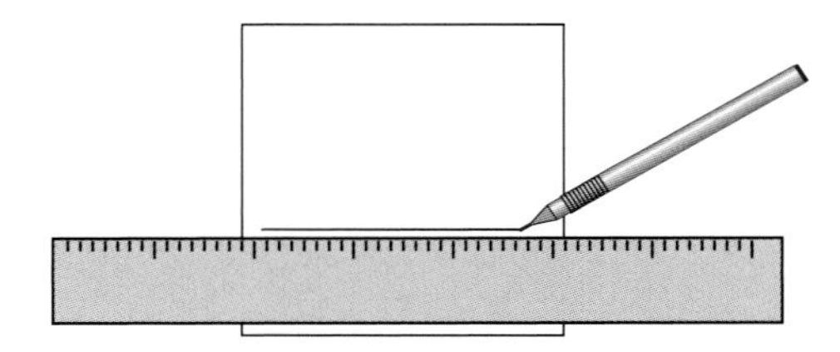

Place the ruler on the card and measure. Per the instructions, divide the horizontal or vertical measurements by the number of rows stated in the instructions. Mark the measured area with a small, light pencil dot.

Another way to sew without measuring is to use the sewing machine's presser foot. The instructions might say to use the presser foot of the sewing machine as a guide, and slowly sew near an edge or a sewn line of stitches. The width of each presser foot might vary from machine to machine. Because of that, the distance of a sewn line might vary for each card, which means that finished cards might differ slightly from maker to maker, making each card unique in its own way.

If sewing by hand, simply sew the new line approximately 1/4 inch (6 mm) from the edge or sewn line. If you are drawing the line, instead of sewing, you can use the 1/4-inch (6 mm) measurement also.

LANDSCAPE VERSUS PORTRAIT

The instructions for each of the cards in this book mention the card format being held as landscape or portrait.

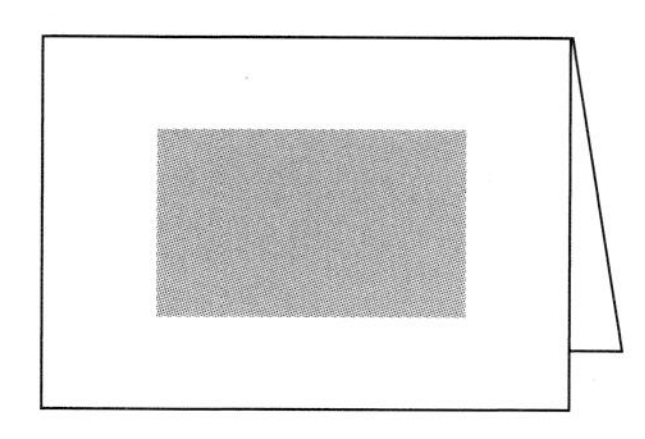

Landscape means that the card is positioned horizontally. The fold will be at the top of the card, so it opens from the bottom up.

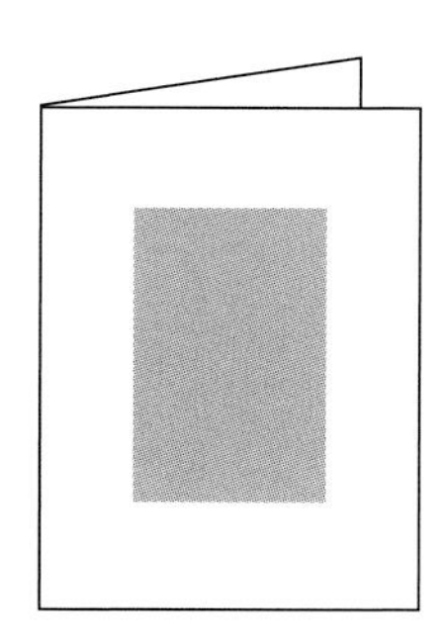

Portrait means the card is positioned vertically. The folded edge will be on the left, and the card will open from the right side.

Square cards can be positioned with the fold of the card on the left so the card will open from the right side, or at the top so it opens from the bottom up.

As you're decorating your card, be sure to remember to open the card so it's flat before you place the objects on the paper, and before you sew.

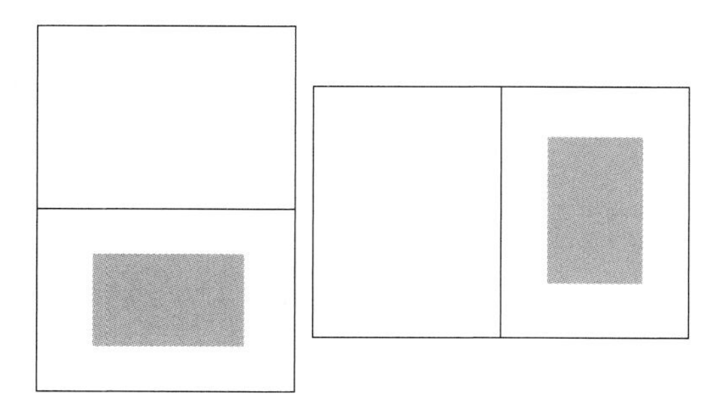

Unless it's mentioned otherwise in the instructions, all cards in the landscape position should have all of the art attached to the bottom area of the folded paper, underneath the crease of the fold. In the portrait position, the art will be attached to the right of the crease of the folded paper.

FINDING MATERIALS

Sometimes you'll find materials to use for decorating your cards and sometimes the materials will find you.

If you shop at craft stores, you'll notice that there are many materials specifically produced and sold for card making. Some of these materials are really interesting and worth purchasing, and some are not. Also, an endless number of free materials are available that you may have never considered using. These materials can be found in different rooms in your home, including the kitchen, the workshop, and the playroom. You can recycle fabric, paper, gift wrap, ribbon, zippers, netting bags from fruit and vegetables bought at a market, and parts of children's games, to name just a few.

Specific materials are suggested for each project in this book, but I also encourage you to look for and collect other materials around you, as they may be useful when making additional cards. I suggest that you follow a few rules when collecting materials: Collect materials that will not spoil, rot, shed, shred, or fall apart; collect materials that are soft or thin enough to sew with a sewing machine or by hand; and collect materials that will not change over time.

Materials that spoil, rot, shed, or fall apart, and which you should not use, include food, most leaves, and flowers. Food, most leaves, and flowers dry up and crumble. I also suggest avoiding materials made with rubber. Rubber tends to dry and crack, or to yellow over time. That includes rubber bands, elastic, and rubber-based items. While some of these materials might look nice on a card in the short term, they won't over time, especially if the receiver of the card wants to keep it as a memento.

KEEPING IT CLEAN

When you choose recycled objects for your card projects, it's really important to use clean materials for many reasons. The first and most important is for your good health, and the second is so you have a clean, professional-looking card. As a rule, if you are using recycled objects, especially objects that come from the kitchen, wash them with soap and water before they leave the kitchen. This is especially important when using sushi grass, which can have bacteria on it after touching raw fish, assuming you are reusing it from a takeout container.

HAND STAMPING

You may remember printing with potatoes or other cut vegetables as a child, but this age-old technique can also be applied to erasers. My early stamping experiences involved teaching disabled adults to decorate curtains by printing with artichokes, mushrooms, grapefruits, and apples. Years later, as I wanted more control over the patterns I was printing on my own, I tried carving rubber erasers with different designs, and I have been stamping with erasers ever since.

RUBBER ERASER STAMPS

If you want to try hand stamping with rubber erasers to decorate your cards, start by assembling the following items:

- Able-Rub or other art gum rubber erasers, 1 x 1 x 1 inch (2.5 x 2.5 x 2.5 cm)
- X-Acto knife with a sharp blade
- Permanent marker
- Rags or paper towels, for cleanup
- Inked stamp pads in various colors
- Scrap paper

You can find the erasers at an art supply store. Because the erasers are inexpensive, I suggest that you buy at least six, because you may want to cut different designs and you may need to experiment with the cutting technique, especially if you are new to making your own stamps.

HAND CUTTING AN ERASER

To prepare your stamp, draw the design on your eraser, using a permanent maker. You can create your own design or trace another copyright-free design. Remember that as you cut, the sections of the eraser that you leave behind will become the stamp design. Cut the eraser carefully, making sure that you leave at least a 1/8-inch (3 mm) space cut between the different parts of the design. You should cut about 1/4 inch (6 mm) deep into the eraser. Please remember to use caution as you use the X-Acto knife, by keeping your fingers away from the direction you're cutting.

Once your design is finished, try stamping it, using an inked stamp pad and scrap paper. Make any corrections as needed. When you are satisfied with your stamp design, wash the eraser crumbs and ink from the eraser and dry it before you start stamping on your card.

The stamps for projects in this book are:

If you are shy about cutting your own stamps, you can buy children's rubber erasers that come in many different shapes, or you can buy premade stamps.

HAND CUTTING A PENCIL ERASER

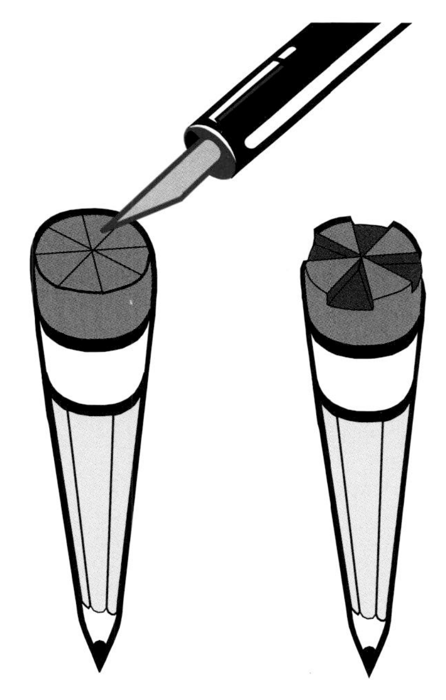

Creating a stamp from a pencil eraser is the same as cutting one from a rubber eraser, except there's not a lot of room for detail in the design. Draw the design on an unused pencil eraser, using an ultrafine permanent marker. Be extra careful as you make the cuts into the eraser with the X-Acto knife, by cutting in a direction away from your body.

HOW TO HAND STAMP

When you are ready to stamp your design on a card, select the stamp and stamp pad color you want to work with.

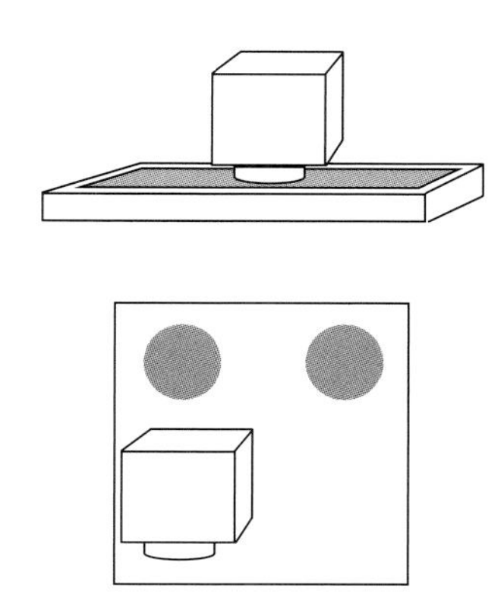

Position the card on the table so it is flat, with the card front facing up. Hold your stamp and press it into the stamp pad. Once the stamp is inked, find the location you want to stamp, and press the inked design-side stamp onto the card.

With a little practice you will learn how much ink you want on the stamp. Unless the instructions specifically say not to, be sure to re-ink the eraser each time you stamp, for fully saturated images.

You can print colors on top of or touching other colors, but you should wait for the first color to dry before applying the second color. If you apply the second color before the first one is dry, you risk having the colors bleed. (On the other hand, you can use this technique on purpose if you like that effect.)

You can also create a mosaic effect by leaving at least 1/8 inch (3 mm) between each shape. You don't need to measure this. Just hold your hand steady, leave a little space, and stamp near the last printed image. Don't worry if the first one looks straight and the next is not. Each stamped image will become part of the larger design, and once the entire pattern is complete, the inconsistencies will become a part of the design and shouldn't be noticeable.

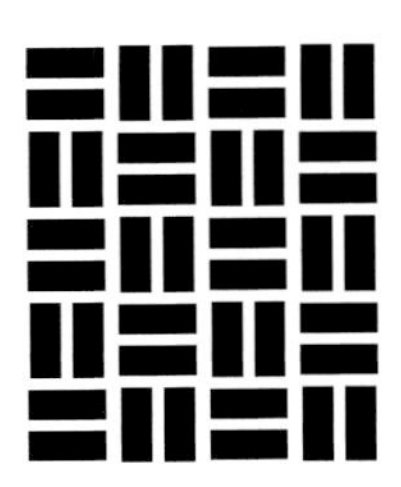

There are many fun things about hand stamping, but what I like most about it is that you can use one stamp to make many different printed designs. You can hold the stamp or object in one direction and stamp the pattern over and over again to get a simple repeat. Or you can rotate it 90 degrees each time you stamp it, or 180 degrees, or you can turn it randomly. The choice of your printed repeat pattern is unlimited and will look great no matter which you choose. In addition, stamping is easy to create, and forgiving if you make mistakes.

When the ink is dry, you can then proceed to the next step in creating your card. Try to be patient while the ink dries. Wet ink will smear all over your sewing machine, on the card stock, and on your hands.

ALUMINUM FOIL AND WAXED PAPER STAMPS

Experiment using both foil and waxed paper stamps. Both offer different effects when printing on different kinds of card stock.

Measure out a 4- to 5-inch (10 to 12.5 cm) piece of aluminum foil or waxed paper. Bunch it up so it is almost a ball shape, pinching the top part so it creates a handle of sorts that can be held with your thumb and forefinger.

Before inking, hold the foil or waxed paper by the handle and press it firmly on your work surface so the bottom flattens out.

Then press the flattened side into the stamp pad. Once the stamp is inked, experiment stamping on a piece of scrap paper with a few presses, to make sure it is nicely inked to your approval.

Re-ink, find the location you want to stamp, and press your stamp on the card. Re-ink and repeat to create a texture or design on the card.

If you want to use foil or waxed paper to stamp a second color, I suggest that instead of cleaning the stamp, that you make a new one for each color. Because they are so easy and inexpensive to make, it is easier to start fresh than wash the first one.

FRUIT AND VEGETABLE PRINTING

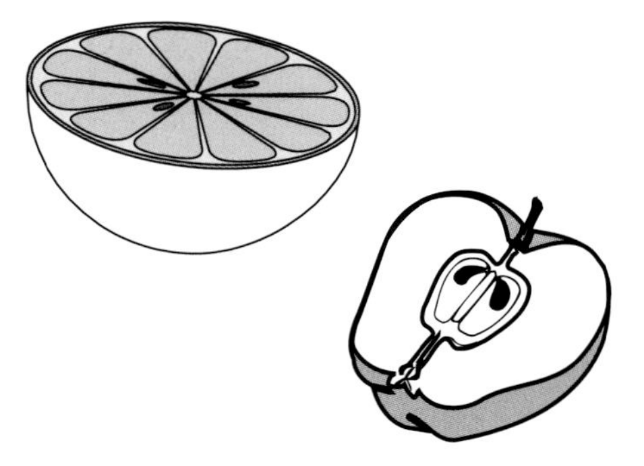

I started printing with fruits and vegetables decades ago, and I still enjoy it.

To do so requires some planning ahead. In my experience, a newly cut piece of fruit or veggie doesn't print very well because its juice makes it too wet to pick up ink or paint.

The day before, choose a piece of fruit or a vegetable that is small enough to fit on your stamp pad. Cut it open with a sharp knife so it has a flat surface for printing, and place it, cut side down, on a paper towel for an hour or more so that some of the moisture soaks into it. Then turn it over and let it air dry overnight, to allow more moisture to evaporate. Depending on the humidity, it should be dry enough on the surface to use as a stamp the next day.

Fruits good for printing are small apples, pears, oranges, lemons, and limes. Good vegetables are small onions, potatoes and radishes (which are also fun to carve), carrots, edible mushrooms, artichokes, and sweet peppers. These are just a few examples. Feel free to try using any reasonably stiff or hard fruits or vegetables. I caution you to stay away from ripe avocados because they can be mushy, and to stay away from just about all watery fruits, such as tomatoes, melons, and grapes.

To print with any fruit or vegetable, press the flat side into the stamp pad. Experiment printing on a scrap piece of paper, inking it a few times before you start, to make sure it is nicely saturated and that you like the pattern it creates.

Re-ink, and press it on the card to create a texture or design on the card.

CRAYON RUBBINGS

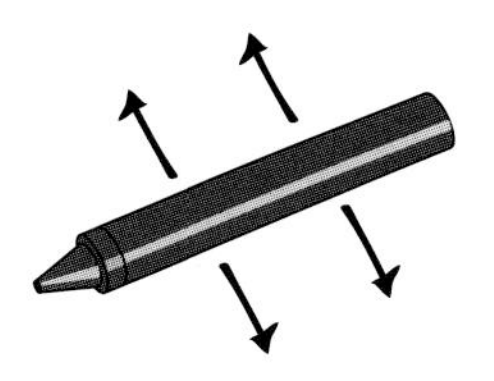

When I was younger, I enjoyed making gravestone rubbings. If you have never tried it, or if you don't remember how to do it, just place a piece of paper over a gravestone, then rub the side of a big crayon over the surface to make a copy of the engraved text or design. Nowadays, gravestone rubbing is frowned upon in many cemeteries, so ask before you try it.

Crayon rubbing techniques can be used to create textures from an unlimited number of objects on paper or fabric. Flat textured items that I enjoy using include car tires, corrugated cardboard, cardboard from children's game parts, tile floors, cast-iron hot-air vents, and any other hard and flat textured objects you see around your home, office, workshop, and yard.

COLORING BETWEEN THE LINES

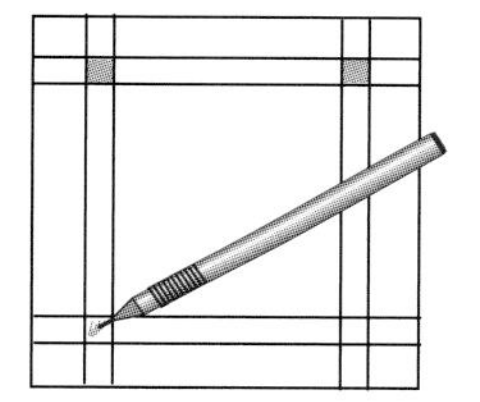

Create a faux patchwork effect without using any fabric: Sew lines of stitches, instead of drawing them, and then color right up to the stitching, inside the different shapes. This technique creates a nice design that has a textured outline.

Thread and markers may be used in an unlimited number of color combinations, but two combinations are my favorite: Fill in the stitched shape with the same color marker as the thread, or stitch with black thread, and then fill in the shape with a contrasting marker color.

It's also fun to combine different surface design techniques. After stamping a pattern of shapes, stitch a number of lines between them. Then color in the newly stitched shapes to further enhance the design.

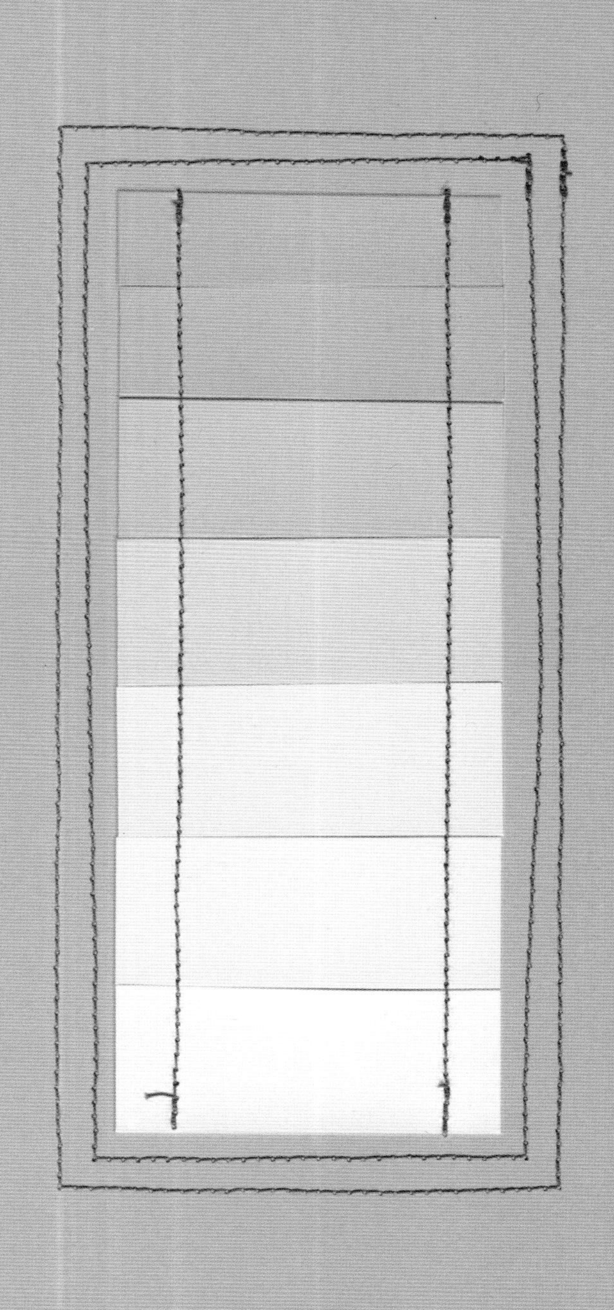

CHAPTER 2

Recycled Objects

When thinking about materials to use when decorating cards, I think it's safe to say that most people would never consider using recycled objects. I encourage you to think about trying new and unusual materials. One way to do it is to start looking at what's around you as you go about your day, considering the design possibilities an object might offer in terms of pattern and color, and then start collecting materials.

Keeping an eye open when in the kitchen is a good place to start. Did your fruit or vegetables come in interesting packaging, such as netting? It can be used as one would use various fabrics, used either in single layers or in many to create a richer color.

Sushi lovers might consider the green plastic grass on the plate to be trash after the meal is over, but it is one of my most favorite objects to recycle and use because of its color and the many design possibilities it offers. If you do use it in a project, please read about cleanliness (page 14) before it goes from the plate to your worktable.

If you frequent coffee shops, or make your own coffee in to-go cups, don't overlook the sleeves that are used around cups to keep from burning your hand. They have a nice corrugated cardboard inside, which can be used as its own design element or as a texture for crayon rubbings as described in the "Surface Design" chapter on page 197.

LOOKING AROUND THE OTHER ROOMS IN YOUR HOUSE . . .

When redecorating, it has always felt wasteful when it came time to throw out the color swatches of the paint. Consider cutting them up and sewing the colored squares to a card.

Anyone who has an old collection of slides of their artwork, or from a collection of family pictures, may have pages and pages of clear slide sheet pages. If you have no idea how to reuse them, consider filling each pocket with something and stitching it to a card. You can also reuse conference name tag badges in a similar way, instead of throwing them out.

Many stores provide really nice, thick plastic bags when making a purchase. A number have bold graphics, such as stripes or circles. Some of the bags are opaque, whereas others are semitransparent. Collect them and consider different ways to cut them up and reuse them.

Craft stores sell beautiful bunches of fabric flowers and leaves, usually on plastic stems or branches. They can be removed from the stems and branches and used on their own. When using as a card decoration, do look for flatter objects instead of lumpier ones.

Ever since seeing it wrapped around building sites while they are being renovated, I've developed a passion for orange construction fencing, and I've been using the textures of them in my artwork for years. Included in this chapter are a few cards that include sewing actual pieces of fencing on the card. It's usually made of a thin plastic and is very easy to machine sew.

Besides what's mentioned here, I encourage you to look around and find more objects to recycle and reuse when making additional cards. Have fun collecting!

Red Netting Red Card

Netting from a produce bag that matches the card color offers fun design possibilities.

MATERIALS

- Rectangular landscape red card stock, folded
- 1 piece of red netting from a produce bag, or red tulle, cut smaller than the actual card size
- 1 strip of fabric or paper that has circles or another graphic pattern, cut smaller than the netting
- Red thread, for sewing
- White thread, for bobbin

INSTRUCTIONS

1. Hold the card open and flat, face up.
2. Place the strip of patterned paper or fabric on the top of the card, centered and a little above top-to-bottom centering (this is called optical center).

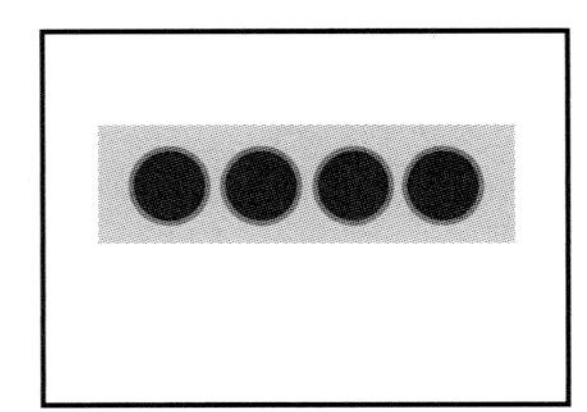

3. Place the piece of red netting on top of the patterned paper or fabric, covering it and centered on the card. Hold both materials in place on the cover of the card.

4. Sew a straight stitch through the netting, slightly tracing the patterned piece of paper or fabric so it is locked in place by the stitching.

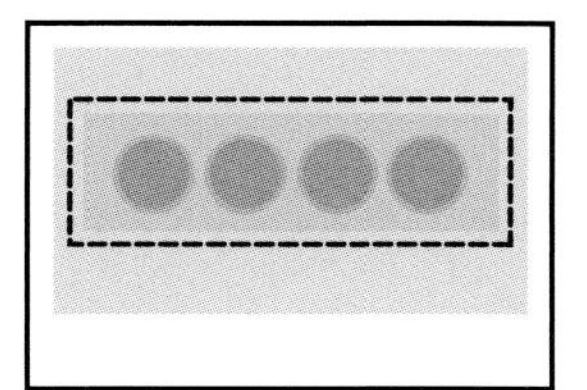

5. Sew a straight stitch around the edge of the red netting, keeping slightly inside of the netting.

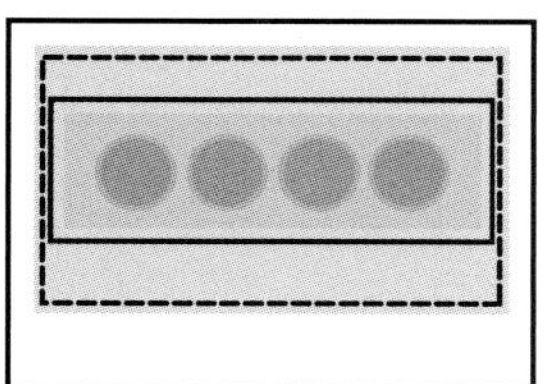

6. Trim the ends of any loose threads on the front and inside of the card.

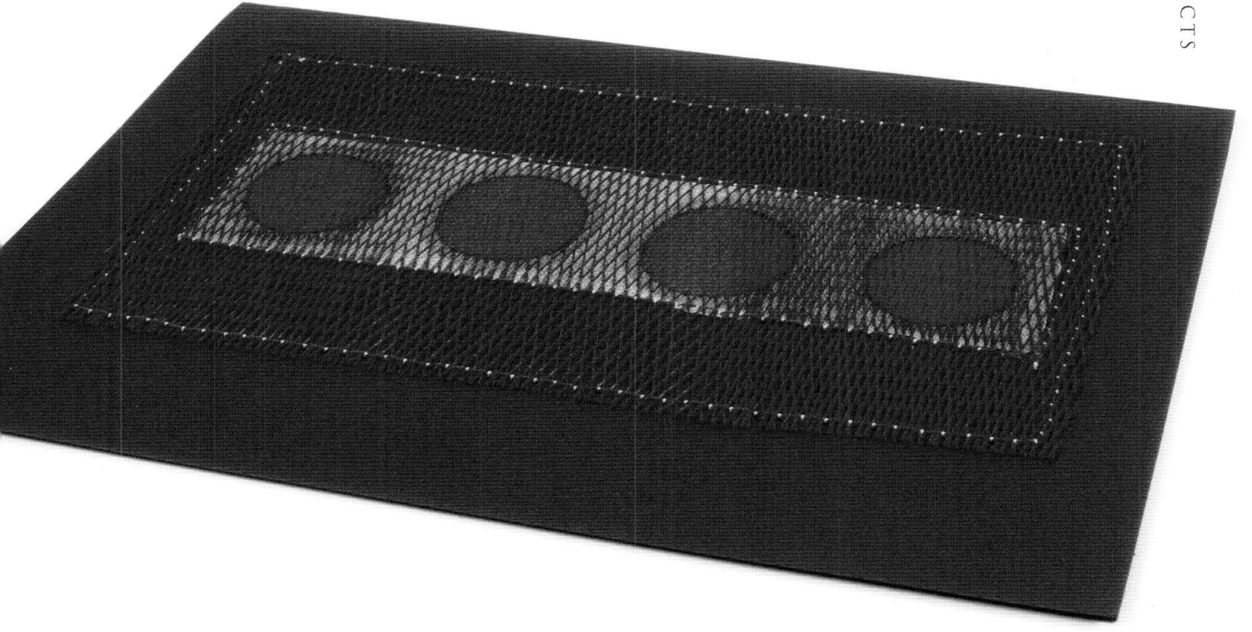

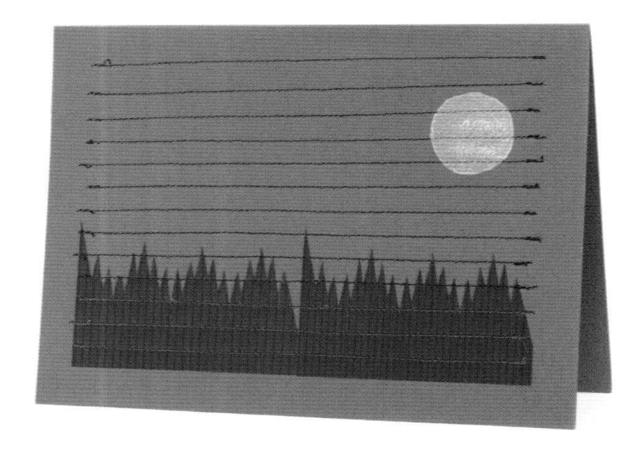

Sushi Grass Landscape

Pieces of sushi grass, lines of thread, and a stamped circle can be used to create a landscape that includes the sky and the moon.

MATERIALS

- Rectangular landscape medium blue card stock, folded
- 2 pieces of sushi grass
- 1 (1 x 1 x 1-inch [2.5 x 2.5 x 2.5 cm]) rubber eraser, cut into a circular shape (see page 14)
- White inked stamp pad
- Green thread, for sewing
- Blue thread, for sewing
- Medium blue thread, for bobbin

INSTRUCTIONS

1. Hold the card open and flat, face up.
2. Place two pieces of sushi grass side by side, centered horizontally a little above the bottom edge of the paper.
3. Using the sewing machine presser foot as a guide, follow the bottom edge of the sushi grass to stitch a straight green line horizontally over the row of sushi grass, to keep it in place.

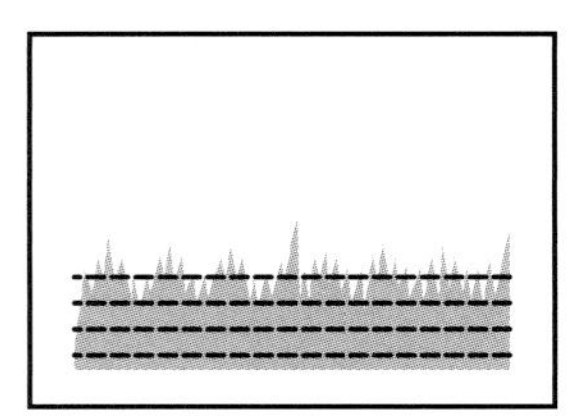

4. Stitch two additional lines over the sushi grass.

5. Stitch additional blue lines on the card, near the top of the sushi grass, continuing to use the presser foot as a guide, stopping and starting at a similar distance from the paper edge as from the sushi grass. When you're finished, there may be plus or minus thirteen stitched lines in total.

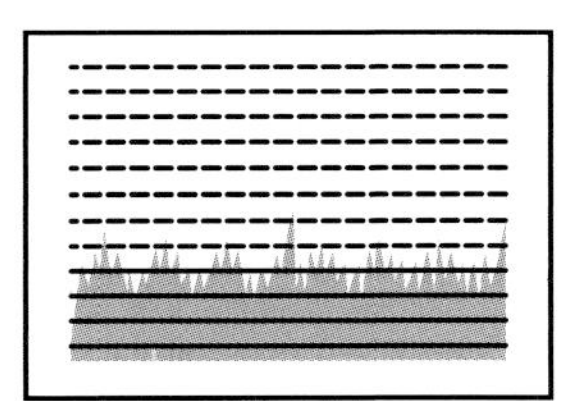

6. Press the circular stamp into the inked stamp pad. Press the inked stamp near the upper right corner of the card stock, over the stitches. Refer to page 15 for technique suggestions. Allow the ink to dry before proceeding.

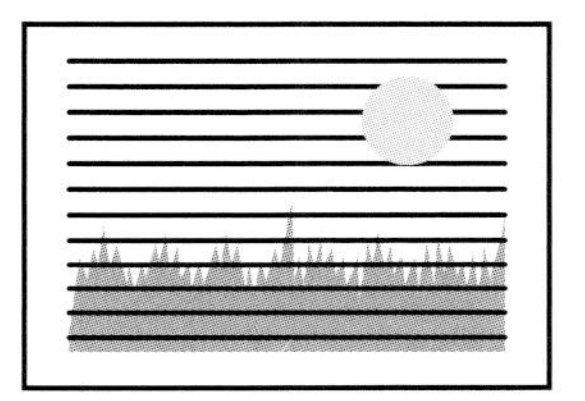

7. Trim the ends of any loose threads on the front and inside of the card.

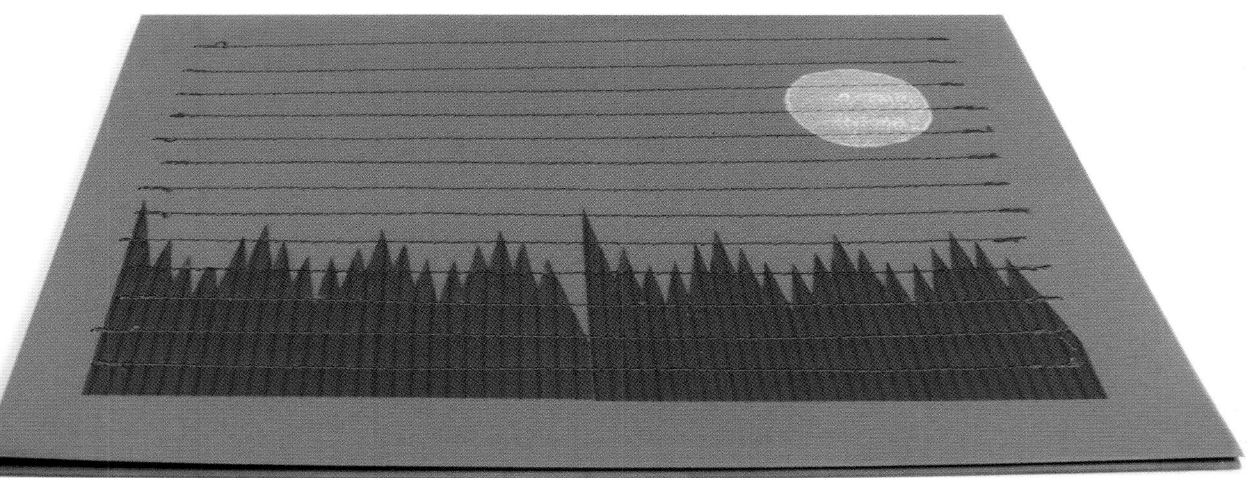

Flower in the Grass

Create your own flower card using sushi grass, a paper or fabric flower, and thread.

MATERIALS

- Rectangular portrait light gray card stock, folded
- 1 piece of sushi grass
- 1 paper or fabric flower
- Green thread, for sewing
- White thread, for sewing and for bobbin
- Optional: Green marker or green colored pencil

INSTRUCTIONS

1. Hold the card open and flat, face up.
2. Center a paper or fabric flower below the top edge of the paper.
3. Using white thread, sew the flower in place slowly, using a zigzag stitch, stopping and turning the card as the edge of the flower turns.
4. Place one piece of sushi grass centered a little above the bottom edge of the paper.

5. Using green thread, sew a straight line horizontally over the bottom edge of sushi grass, to hold it in place.

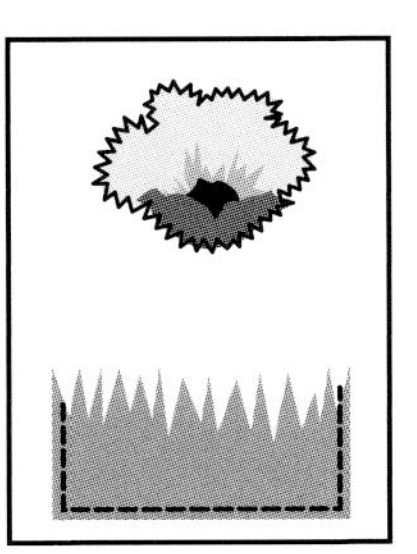

6. Starting at the bottom edge of the sushi grass, sew two slightly curved straight lines up to the bottom edge of the flower, keeping the lines parallel to each other, to create the stem. Sew a leaf to the left of the stem and another to the right.

7. Trim the ends of any loose threads on the front and inside of the card.

8. Color in the leaves and stem, using a green marker or colored pencil, if you wish.

Light to Dark Paint Swatches

After choosing paint colors, put the paint swatches to new use.

MATERIALS

- Rectangular portrait curry yellow card stock, folded
- 1 paint store swatch strip with 6 or more colors
- Orange thread, for sewing
- Yellow thread, for bobbin

INSTRUCTIONS

1. Hold the card open and flat, face up.
2. Cut each color on the strip of paint swatches into pieces. Discard the white space between colors.
3. Trim the colors in rectangles, discarding the printed text.

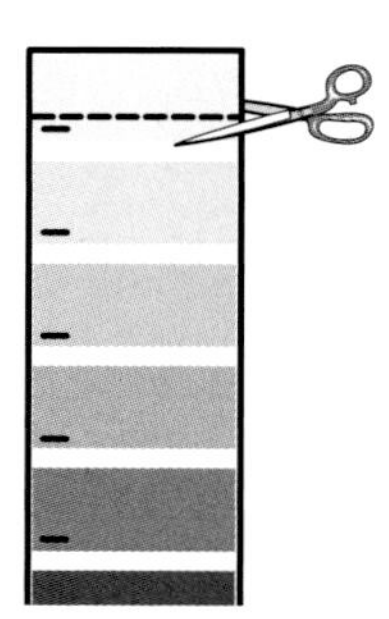

4. Line up the colors from dark to light on a work surface.

5. Compare the length of the line of the colored pieces to the length of the card.
6. Center and place the darkest color near the top of the card, leaving enough length for all of the pieces to line up close to being centered vertically.

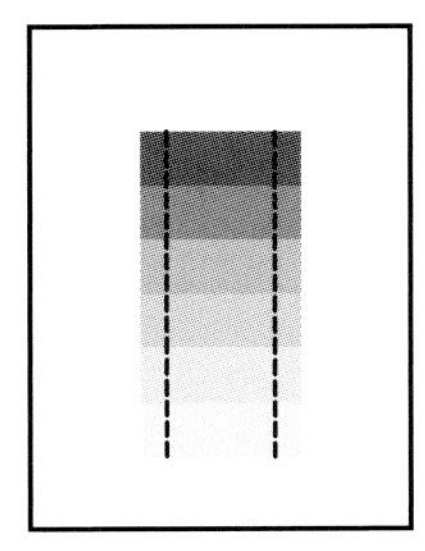

7. Using the presser foot of the sewing machine as a guide, slowly sew near the right edge of the first color, adding the next lighter color as you sew the darker one before it. Repeat for all six or more pieces.
8. Using the presser foot as a guide, sew near the left edge of the line of colors.
9. Using your presser foot as a guide once again, stitch around the outside edge of the stitched line of colored pieces, creating a box around the line of color.

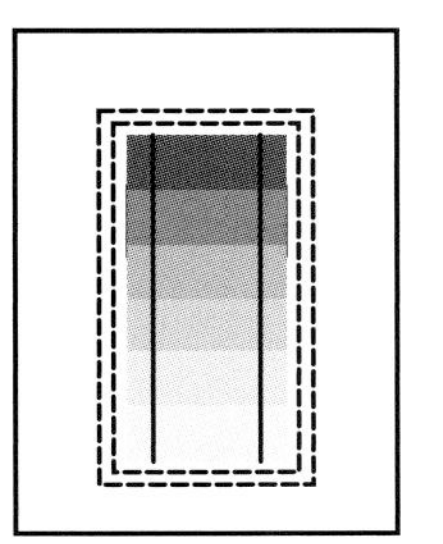

10. Stitch again inside the stitched box, to create a new box inside the outer box.
11. Trim the ends of any loose threads on the front and inside of the card.

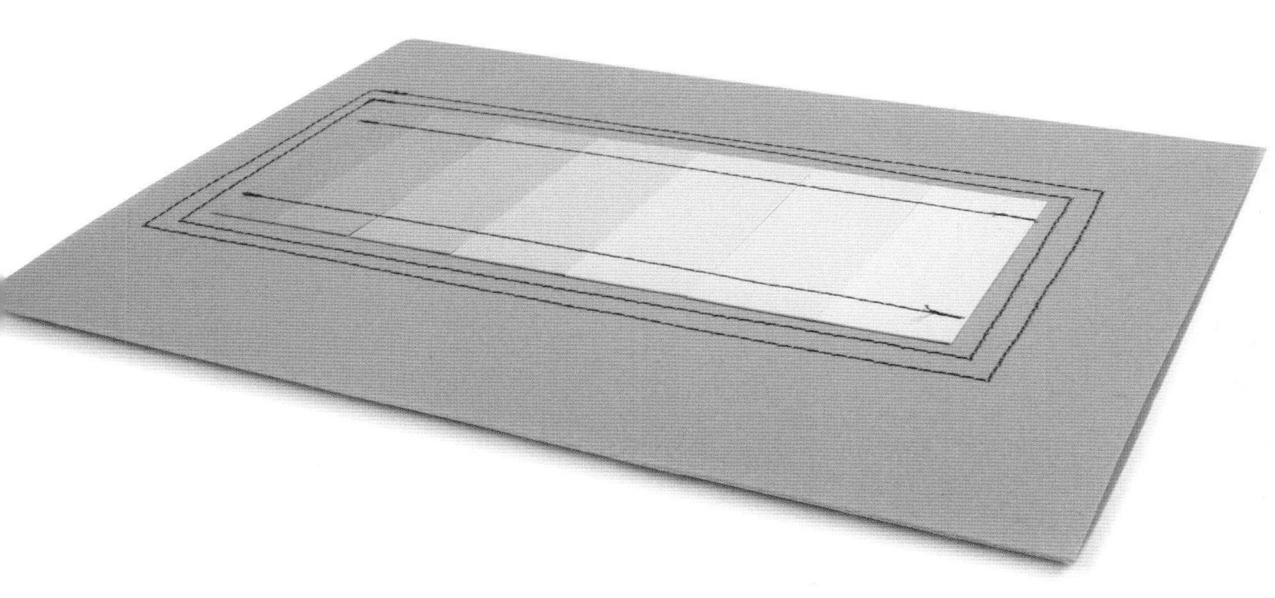

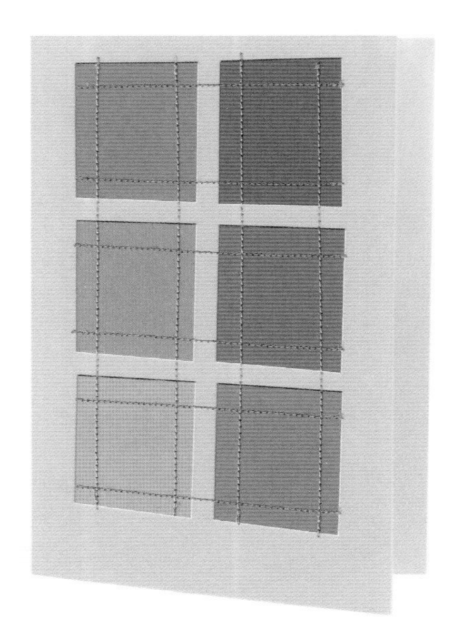

Orange Paint Swatches

Create a patchwork quilt–like card with orange paint swatches, instead of with fabric.

MATERIALS

- Rectangular portrait turquoise card stock, folded
- 2 paint swatch cards with 3 colors each
- Turquoise thread, for sewing and bobbin

INSTRUCTIONS

1. Hold the card open and flat, face up.
2. Cut each color on the two paint swatch strips into three pieces each. Discard the white space between colors.
3. Trim each color into squares, discarding the excess.

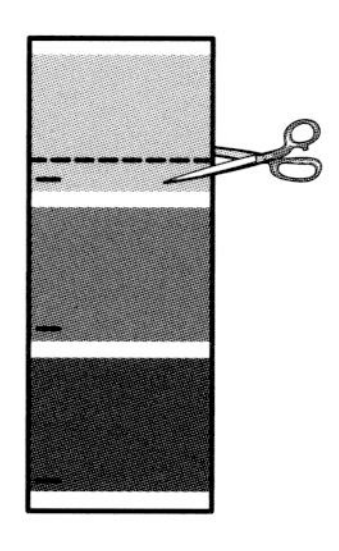

4. On your work surface, line up the square colors from each cut strip from dark to light in two separate vertical rows.

5. Center and place the darkest piece from the first paint strip near the top right of the center of the card, leaving enough length for all of the pieces to be stitched vertically.

6. Using the presser foot of the sewing machine as a guide, slowly sew the left edge of the first color. Stitch the next two pieces in place on the right column, spacing each piece about 1/4 inch (6 mm) apart.

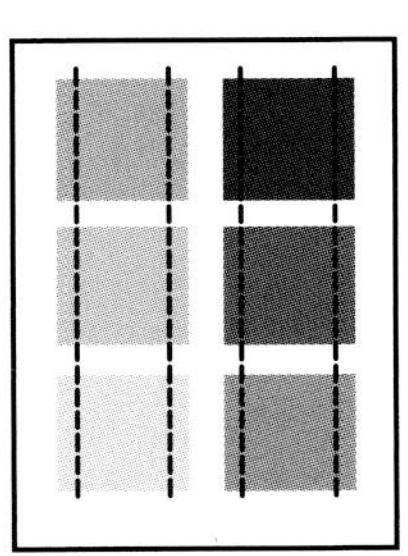

7. Repeat by sewing the three pieces from the second strip on the left side of center, using the presser foot as a guide on the right side of the column.

8. Sew the outer edges of both columns.

9. Stitch the top and bottom edges of each of the three rows of squares.

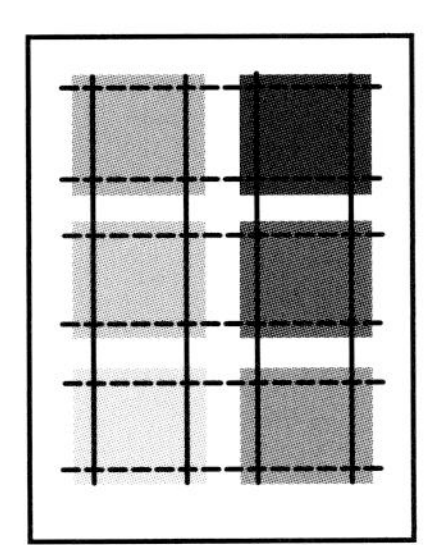

10. Trim the ends of any loose threads on the front and inside of the card.

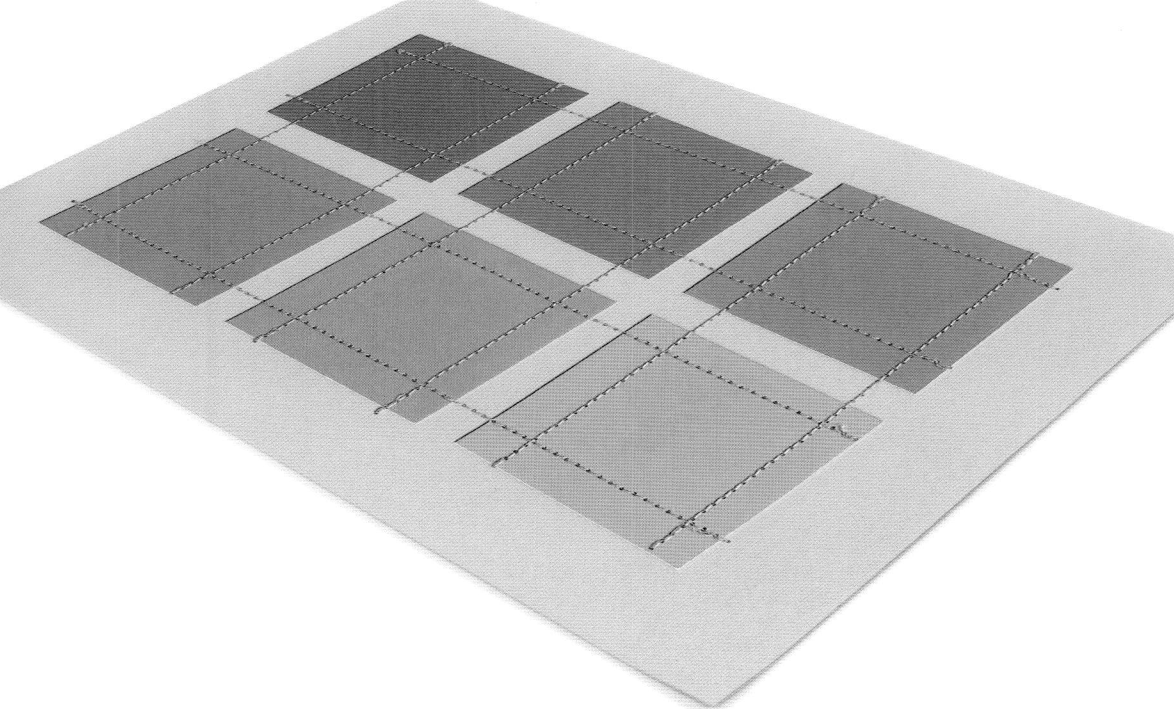

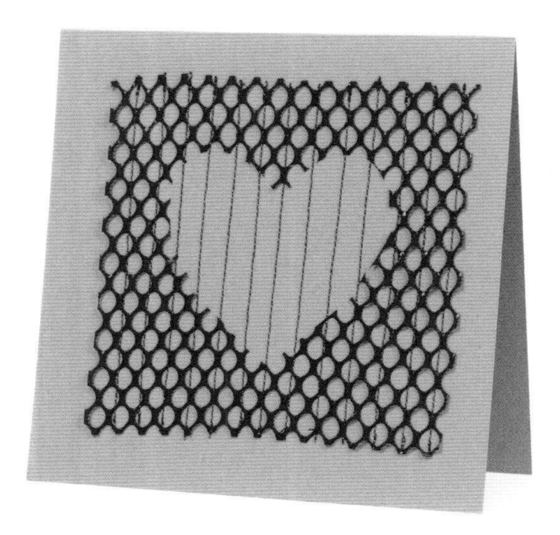

Inside-Out Heart

The netting covering clementine boxes is fabriclike and fun to work with.

MATERIALS

- Square lilac card stock, folded
- 1 large piece of red netting from a box of clementines
- Red thread, for sewing
- Lilac thread, for bobbin

INSTRUCTIONS

1. Hold the card open and flat, face up.
2. Measure and cut a square piece of netting that is slightly smaller than the card.
3. Fold the square in half and cut a heart shape from the center, being sure to leave some netting at the top and bottom so the square remains as one piece.

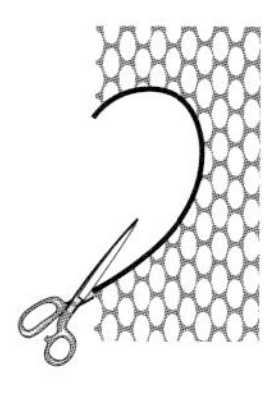

4. Open the square and place in the center of the card.

5. Sew a straight line from the top center of the netting, over the netting, through the empty heart space, and over the netting again to the bottom of the netting.

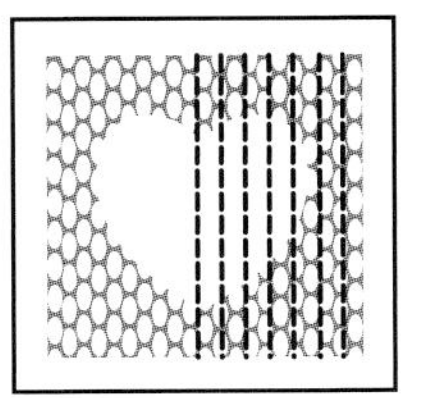

6. Using the presser foot of the sewing machine as a guide, sew additional lines to the right of the first line, until the right side is attached to the card.

7. Repeat, using the presser foot of the sewing machine as a guide, sewing additional lines to the left of the first line, until the left side is attached to the card.

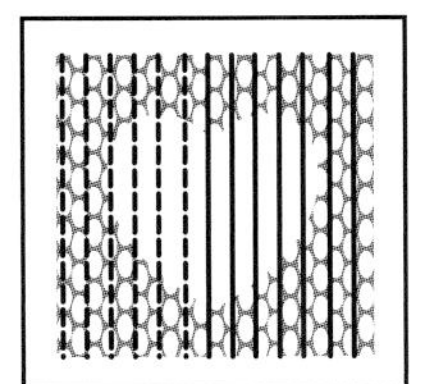

8. Trim the ends of any loose threads on the front and inside of the card.

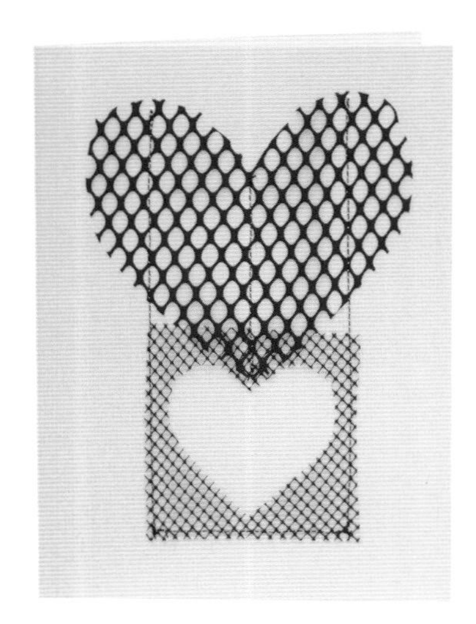

Positive and Negative Heart Shapes

Try working with positive and negative heart shapes. Don't throw the empty heart shape away. Use it in your design.

MATERIALS

- Rectangular portrait off-white card stock, folded
- 1 large piece of red netting from a box of clementines
- 1 small piece of red netting that's a different pattern from the clementine netting
- Red thread, for sewing
- White thread, for bobbin

INSTRUCTIONS

1. Hold the card open and flat, face up.
2. Measure and cut a square piece of clementine netting that is slightly smaller than the width of the card.
3. Fold the square in half and cut a heart shape from the center.

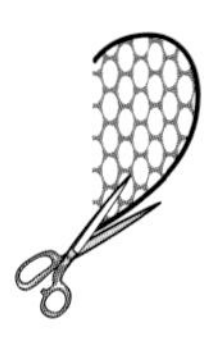

4. Open the heart and place in upper center of card.
5. Cut a square piece of netting that is smaller than the size of the clementine netting heart.

6. Fold the square in half and cut a heart shape from the center, being sure to leave some netting at the top and bottom so the square remains as one piece. Discard the heart shape.

7. Open the square and place in the center of the card, overlapping the bottom point of the heart with the upper point of the square from which the heart has been removed.

8. Sew a straight line from the top center of the heart, down to the top of the overlapping square netting, ending at the bottom of the heart point.

9. Sew an additional line to the right of the first sewn line, starting at the top rounded part of the heart, down the right edge of the square netting, ending at the bottom.

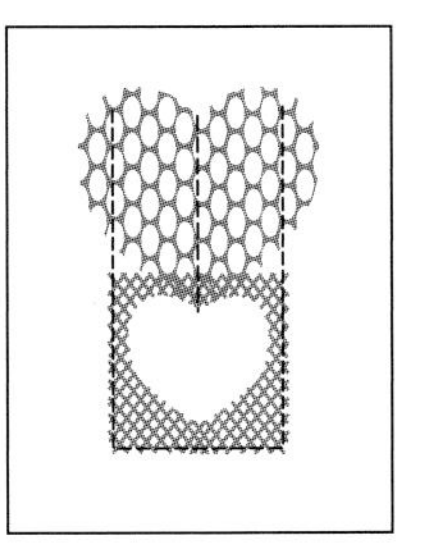

10. Repeat by sewing an additional line to the left of the first line.

11. Sew the bottom of the netting square to attach to the card.

12. Trim the ends of any loose threads on the front and inside of the card.

Seed Packs

Recycle old 35 mm slide pages by filling them with birdseed or seeds for planting.

MATERIALS

- Square yellow-gold card stock, folded
- 1 clear page for 35 mm slides, trimmed to 2 rows of 2 columns
- Birdseed or plant seed (I used thistle seed, which finches love)
- 2 pieces of black patterned yarn
- Yellow-gold thread, for sewing and bobbin

INSTRUCTIONS

1. Hold the card open and flat, face up.
2. Add seeds to each of the four pockets in the slide sheet, where the slide would usually go, being careful not to overfill.
3. Stitch each row of pockets closed.

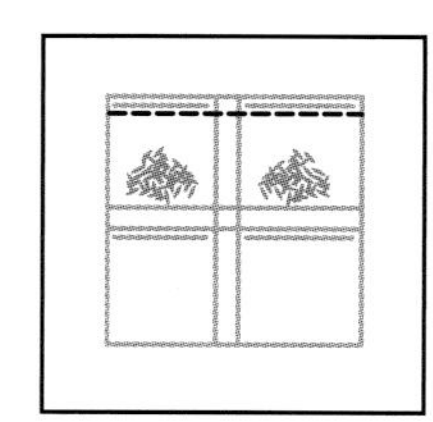

4. Center the pocket-filled slide sheet on the card and stitch the top edge, and then stitch between the two columns in the center. Continue by stitching the right and left edges, then the bottom edge. Finish by sewing between the two rows. Note: The plastic is slippery, so take your time and be sure to hold it flat before stitching.

5. Stitch a piece of yarn above and below the slide sheet, placing it close to the outer edge.

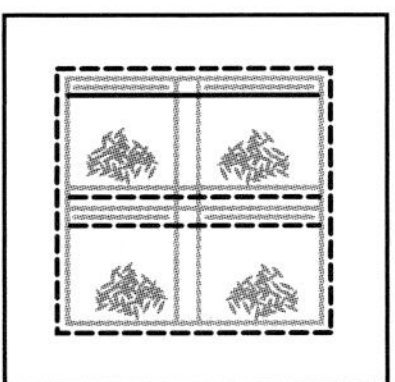

6. Trim the ends of any loose threads on the front and inside of the card.

Three Leaves

Create a card that incorporates the organic shape and texture of leaves with the texture of stitching.

MATERIALS

- Rectangular landscape brown card stock, folded
- 3 decorative leaves, hard stems trimmed and removed (or substitute paper or fabric leaves)
- Green thread, for sewing
- Brown thread, for bobbin

INSTRUCTIONS

1. Hold the card open and flat, face up.
2. Place one leaf in the center of the card so the leaf is on the top part of the opened card with the point toward the fold. Stitch over the center vein.

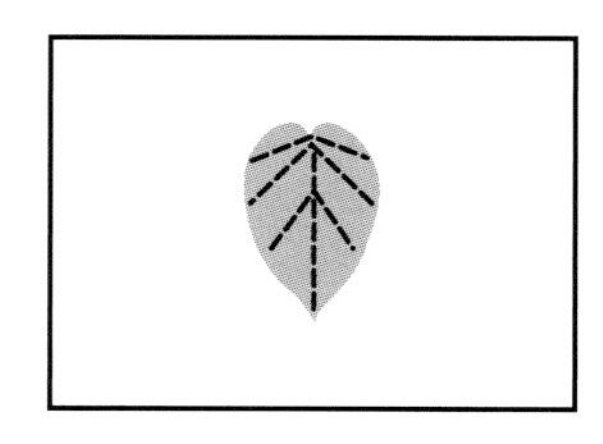

3. Stitch the other veins of the leaf, going from the center of the leaf toward the outer edges. Note: The leaves may be wavy, so pay attention to how they are stitched on the card.

4. Position leaves to the right and left of the first leaf, and stitch the veins.

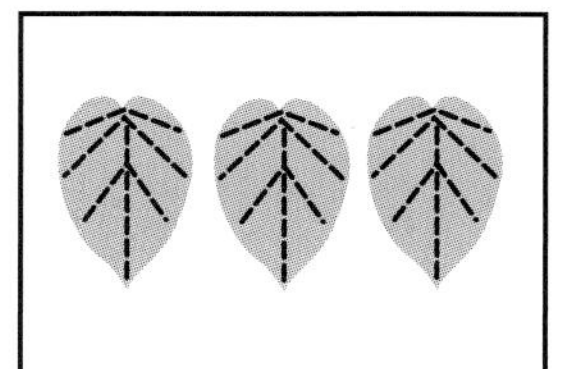

5. Turn the card 180 degrees, so the leaves are point side up and the art is at the bottom of the opened card.

6. Using the sewing machine presser foot as a guide, stitch three rows of stitches following the bottom edge of the card, and two rows of stitches following the crease at the top of the card.

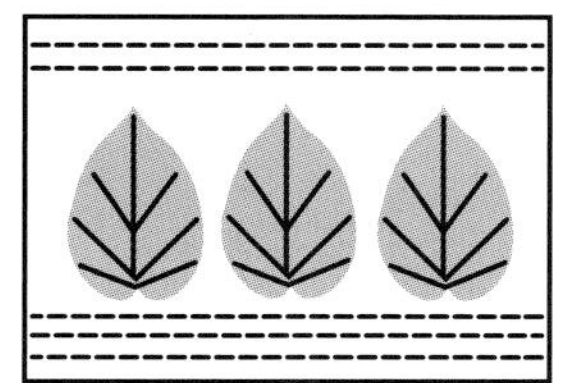

7. Trim the ends of any loose threads on the front and inside of the card.

NOTE: *See page 10 about how to write on a dark-colored card.*

Mirrored(ish) Leaves

Mirrored purple leaves on the diagonal, with a twist.

MATERIALS

- Square green card stock, folded
- 2 decorative purple (or other color) leaves, hard stems trimmed and removed (or substitute paper or fabric leaves)
- 2 pieces of black string or black yarn
- Purple thread, for sewing
- Black thread, for sewing
- Green thread, for bobbin

INSTRUCTIONS

1. Hold the card open and flat, face up.
2. Position one leaf in the upper right with the point near the corner of the card. Stitch purple thread over the center vein.

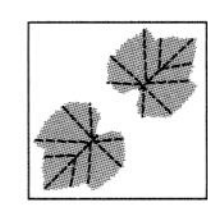

3. Stitch the other veins of the leaf, going from the center of the leaf toward the outer edges.

4. Position the second leaf in the bottom left with the point near the corner. Stitch the veins.

5. Position one piece of string at the end of one leaf, where the stem would go. Using black thread, zigzag stitch over the black string, to hold it in place.

6. Repeat by sewing a piece of string to the second leaf.

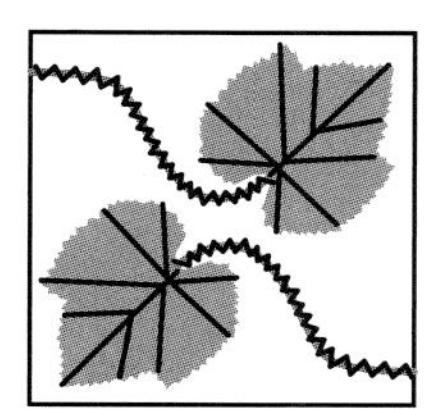

7. Trim the ends of the string and also any loose threads on the front and inside of the card.

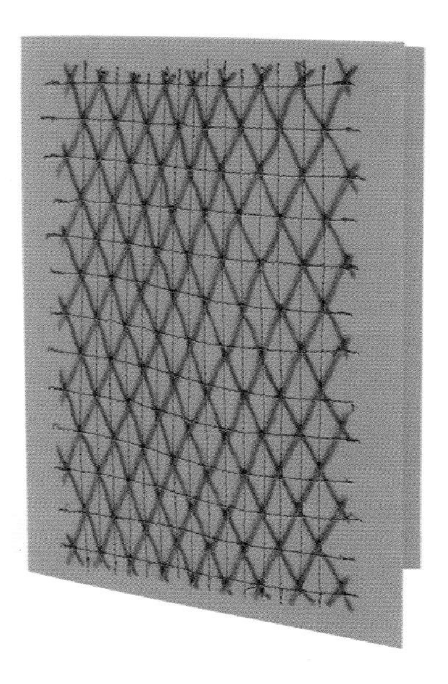

Plaid Variation

The netting protecting a wine bottle was begging to be used in an art project.

MATERIALS

- Rectangular portrait gray card stock, folded
- 1 piece of green netting (check the packaging for wine or liquor bottles)
- Orange thread, for sewing
- Fuchsia thread, for sewing
- Gray thread, for bobbin

INSTRUCTIONS

1. Hold the card open and flat, face up.
2. Trim a piece of green netting so it is smaller than the card size.
3. Center the netting on the card. Stitch orange thread in the center of the net from top to bottom, stitching across the diagonal grid of the net, attaching it in place.

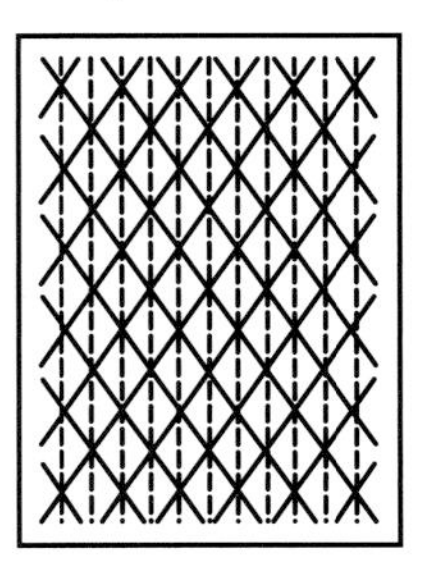

4. Stitch fuchsia thread, starting to the left of the orange thread, sewing from top to bottom from the right side to the left.
5. Turn the card sideways, so the art is at the bottom of the opened card.
6. Starting at the center, near the fold, sew two rows of fuchsia thread at both the far left and far right of the netting.
7. Change to orange thread and sew two rows on the left and right sides, moving toward the middle.
8. Alternate between fuchsia and orange thread as you sew two rows at a time.

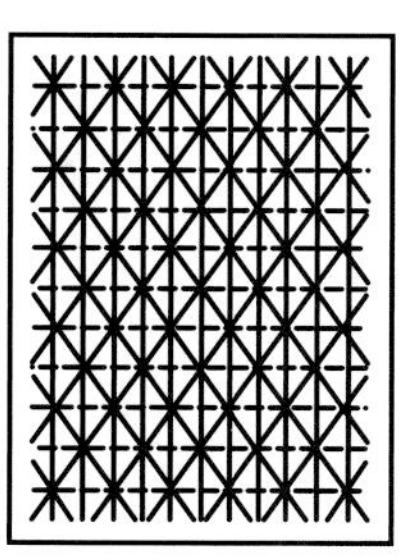

9. If there is an extra row when you get to the center, sew one in the alternate color.
10. Trim the ends of any loose threads on the front and inside of the card.

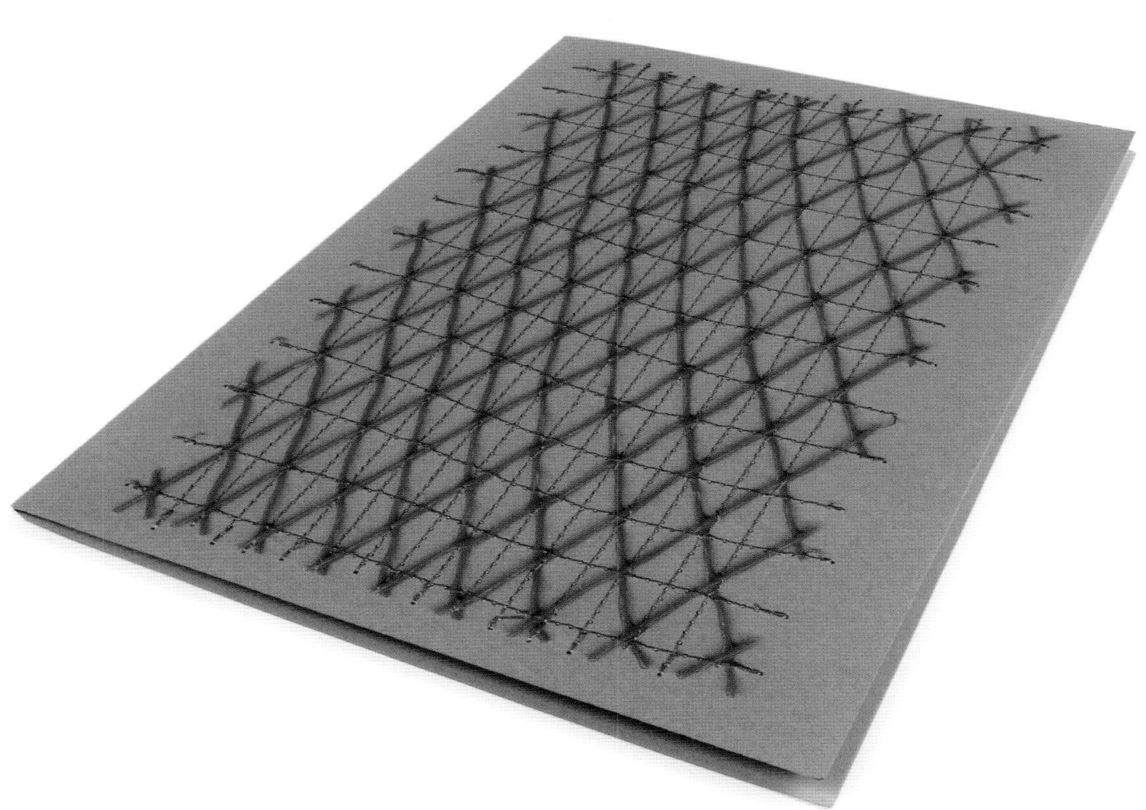

White Abstract on Black

The netting used for garlic bags is finer than citrus bag netting, making it behave almost like tulle.

MATERIALS

- Rectangular portrait black card stock, folded
- 1 piece of white garlic bag netting (or substitute white tulle or fine netting in a different color)
- Black thread, for sewing and bobbin

INSTRUCTIONS

1. Hold the card open and flat, face up.
2. Place the unopened, double-layered white garlic bag across the middle of the card, with the open edge of the bag near one edge of the card. Don't be concerned if its shape isn't straight or if it's folded or overlaps.
3. Following both edges of the white netting, stitch in place, and trim the netting near both edges of the card.

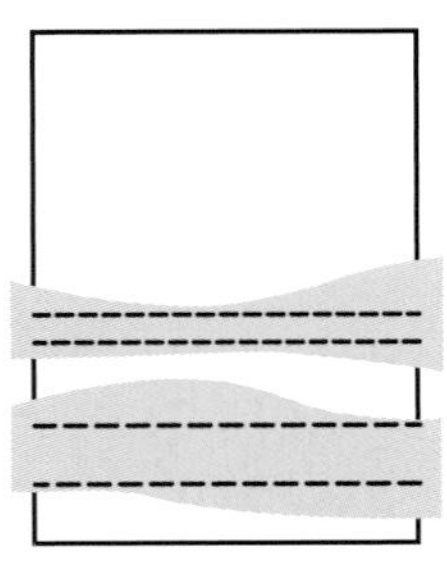

4. Place the rest of the garlic bag across the card, slightly below the netting just sewn.

5. Stitch and trim.

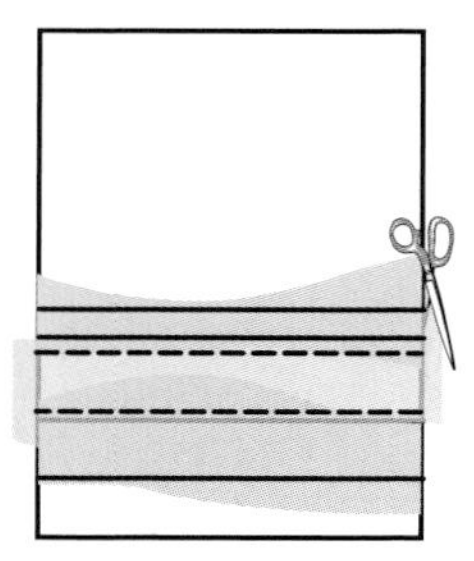

6. Take the leftover white netting and cut the loop to open it, so it's one layer.

7. Position the opened, one-layer piece of netting over the space between the two stitched rows.

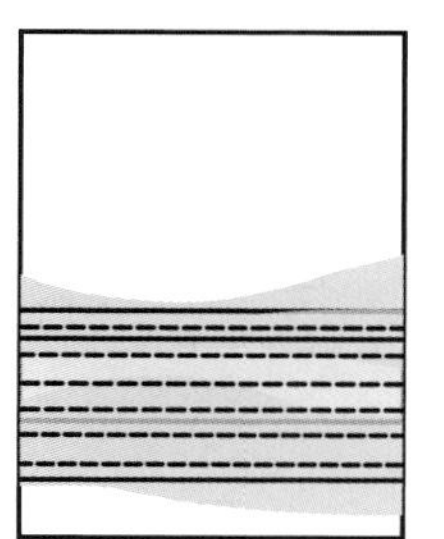

8. Stitch and trim.

9. Stitch random straight lines horizontally across the card, to flatten the three layers of lumpy netting.

10. Trim the netting and the ends of any loose threads on the front and inside of the card.

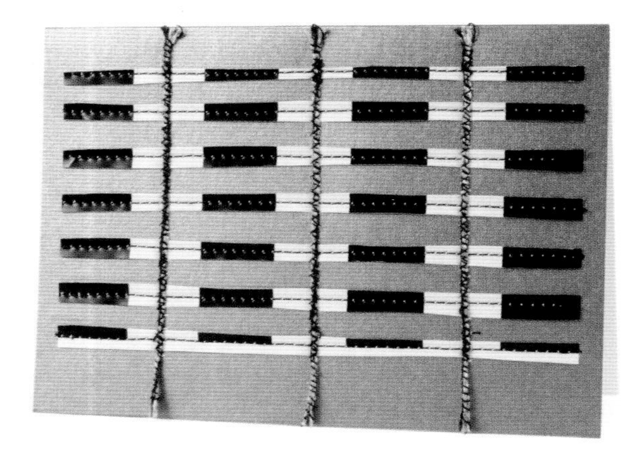

Vertical and Horizontal Stripes

Plastic shopping bags, especially those with black and white stripes, offer many design possibilities.

MATERIALS

- Rectangular landscape metallic gold card stock, folded
- 1 piece of a striped plastic shopping bag (I used a DSW bag; or substitute black-and-white striped fabric or paper)
- 3 pieces of black-and-white string or yarn longer than the height of the card
- Ruler
- X-Acto knife
- Black thread, for sewing
- White thread, for bobbin

INSTRUCTIONS

1. Hold the card open and flat, face up.
2. Cut a piece of plastic bag with black and white stripes so it is smaller than the size of the card front.
3. Center the plastic on the card front, with the stripes in the vertical position.
4. Using the sewing machine presser foot as a guide, stitch from one side of the plastic to the other, across the top of the plastic.

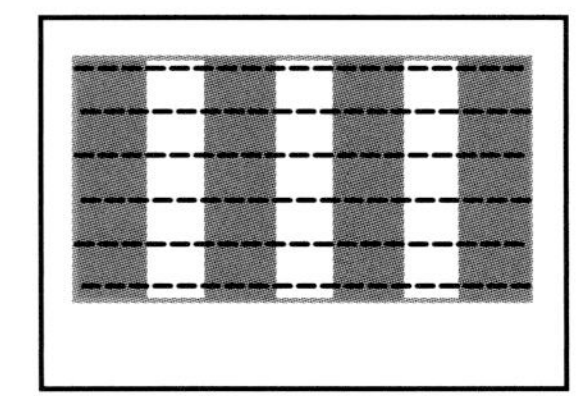

5. Stitch additional rows across the plastic, so it is attached to the card.

6. Using a ruler and an X-Acto knife, carefully cut away the plastic from between each of the rows of stitching. Use enough pressure to cut the plastic, but not into the card. Cut close to the stitches but don't cut them.

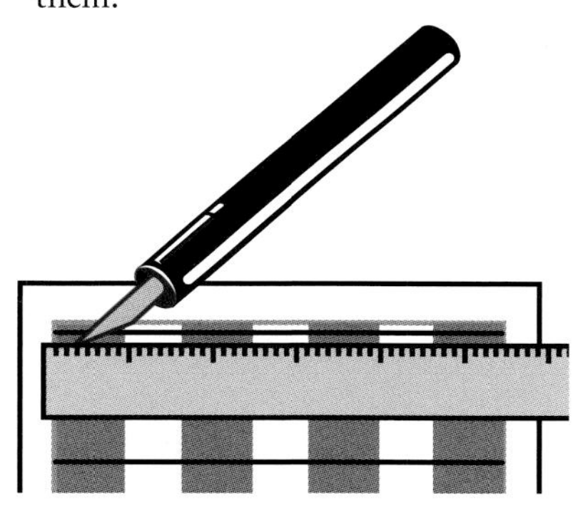

7. Place one of the pieces of string vertically over the left white vertical stripe.

8. Starting at the top of the piece of plastic and ending at the bottom, sew a zigzag stitch over the string, to hold it in place.

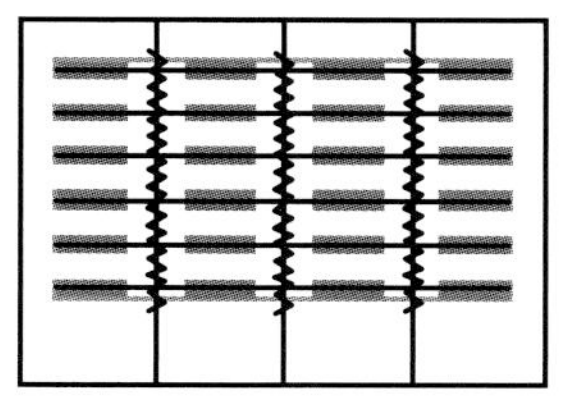

9. Repeat by sewing the next two pieces of string in place over the white vertical strips.

10. Trim the ends of the three pieces of string, and also any loose threads on the front and inside of the card.

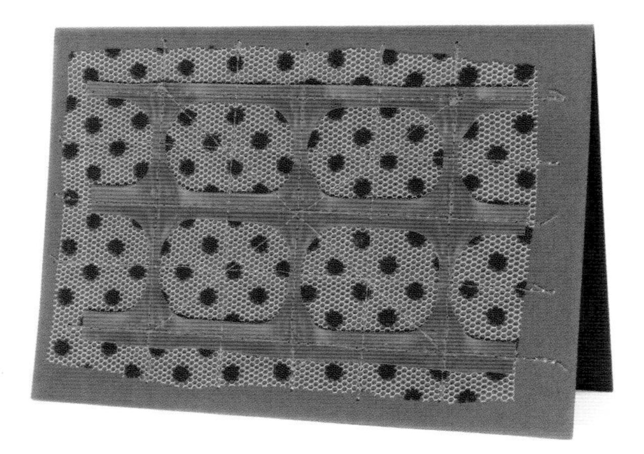

Orange Fence with Black Dots

Don't let the orange fencing from your construction project go to waste. Doll it up with tulle!

MATERIALS

- Rectangular landscape blue card stock, folded
- 1 piece of polka-dotted white or plain tulle
- 1 piece of orange construction fencing
- Orange thread, for sewing
- Blue thread, for bobbin

INSTRUCTIONS

1. Hold the card open and flat, face up.
2. Cut a piece of tulle so it is smaller than the size of the card front. Don't worry if the shape is uneven.
3. Cut a piece of orange construction fencing so it is smaller than the size of the tulle.
4. Place the tulle on the card front and the fencing on top of it.

5. Stitch horizontally from one side of the tulle, over the fencing, and end at the other side of the tulle.

6. Repeat by stitching vertically from the top of the tulle, over the fencing, to the bottom of the tulle.

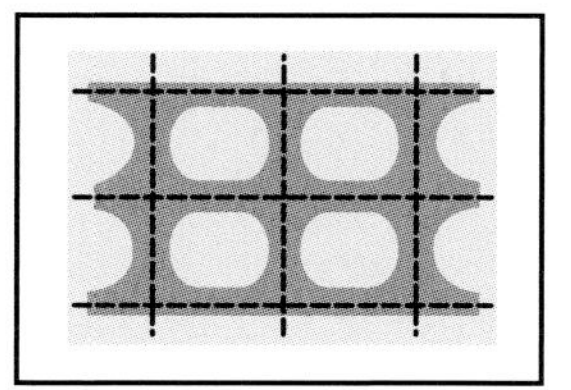

7. Stitch both horizontally and vertically over the tulle and through the holes in the fencing.

8. Stitch diagonally across the fencing, to create more geometry.

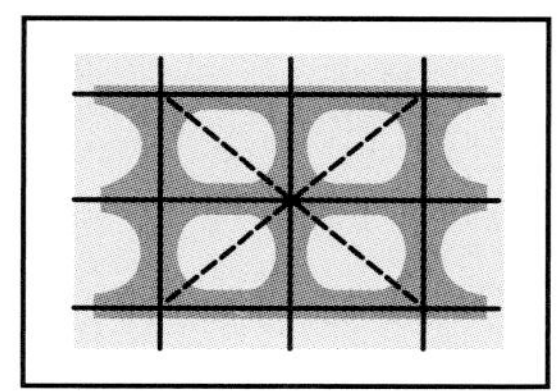

9. Trim the ends of any loose threads on the front and inside of the card.

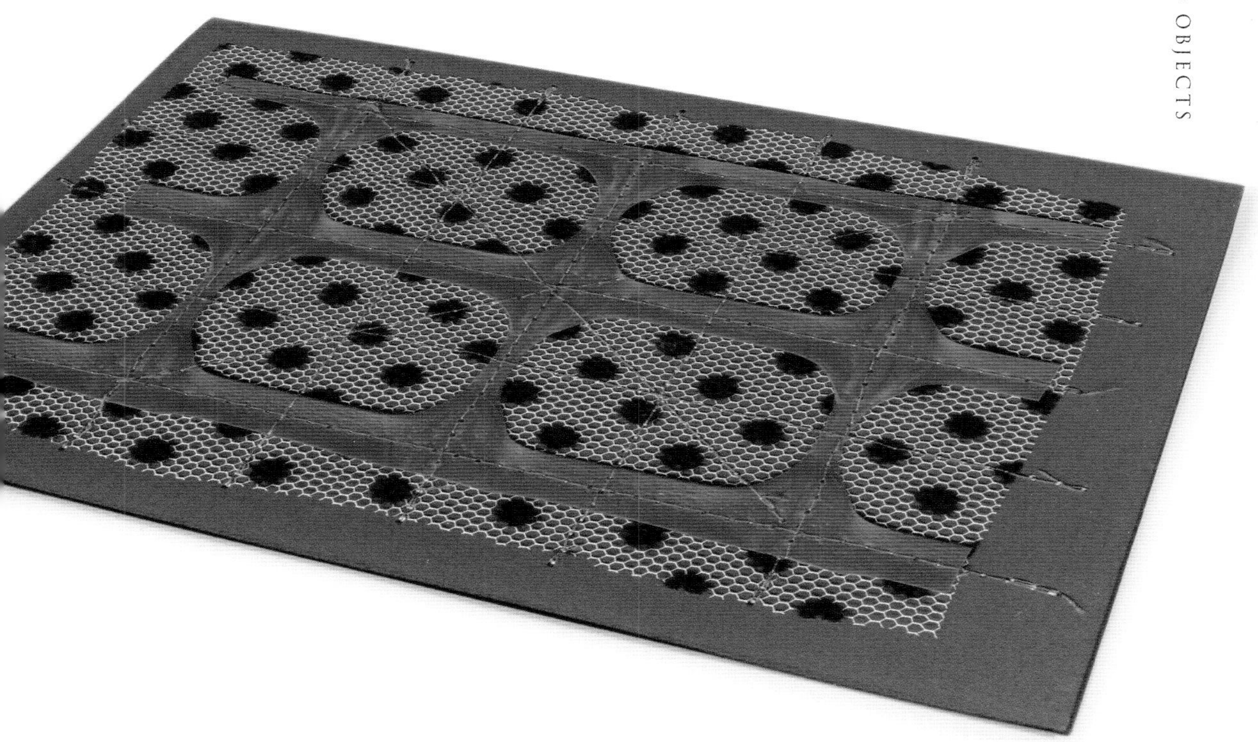

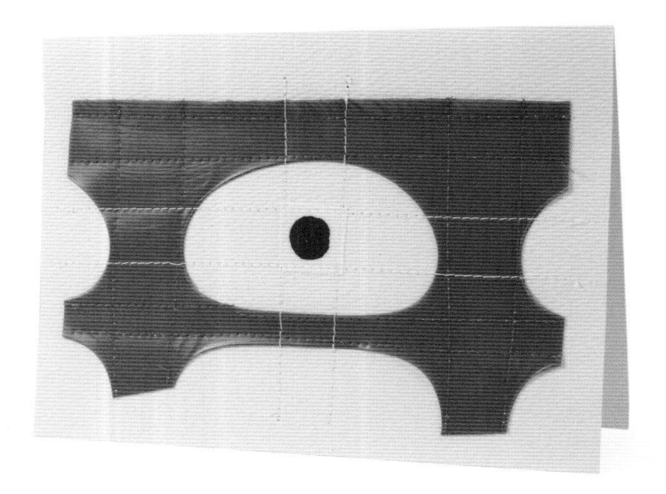

Orange Fence Section with One Red Dot

A cut piece of orange fencing becomes almost unrecognizable with a red dot in the center.

MATERIALS

- Rectangular landscape off-white card stock, folded
- 1 small square piece of dotted white fabric or other patterned fabric
- 1 piece of orange construction fencing
- Orange thread, for sewing
- White thread, for sewing and bobbin

INSTRUCTIONS

1. Hold the card open and flat, face up.
2. Cut one piece of piece of orange construction fencing so it is smaller than the size of the card.
3. Place the piece of fencing centered on the card front.
4. Stitch with orange thread both horizontally and vertically the fencing.

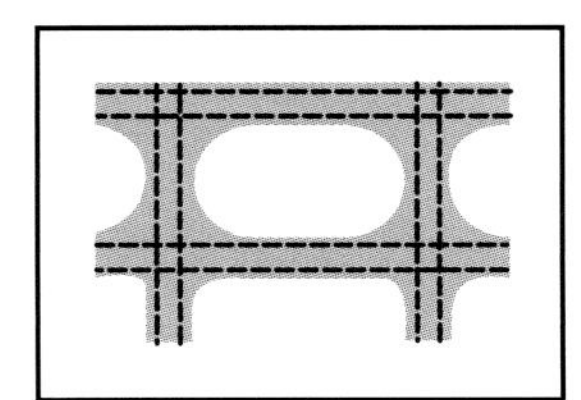

5. Place the square piece of cotton fabric with the dot in the middle of the hole in the fencing.

6. Stitch with white thread both horizontally and vertically through the hole in the fencing, attaching the white square in the process.

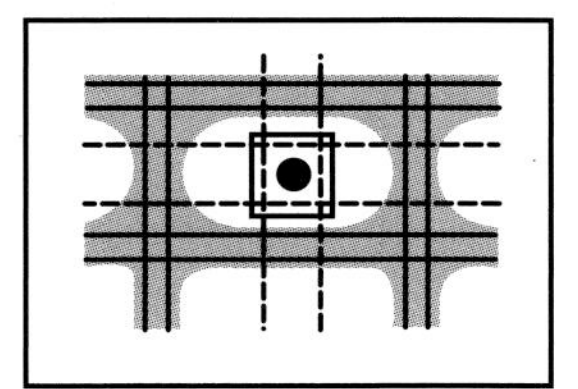

7. Trim the ends of any loose threads on the front and inside of the card.

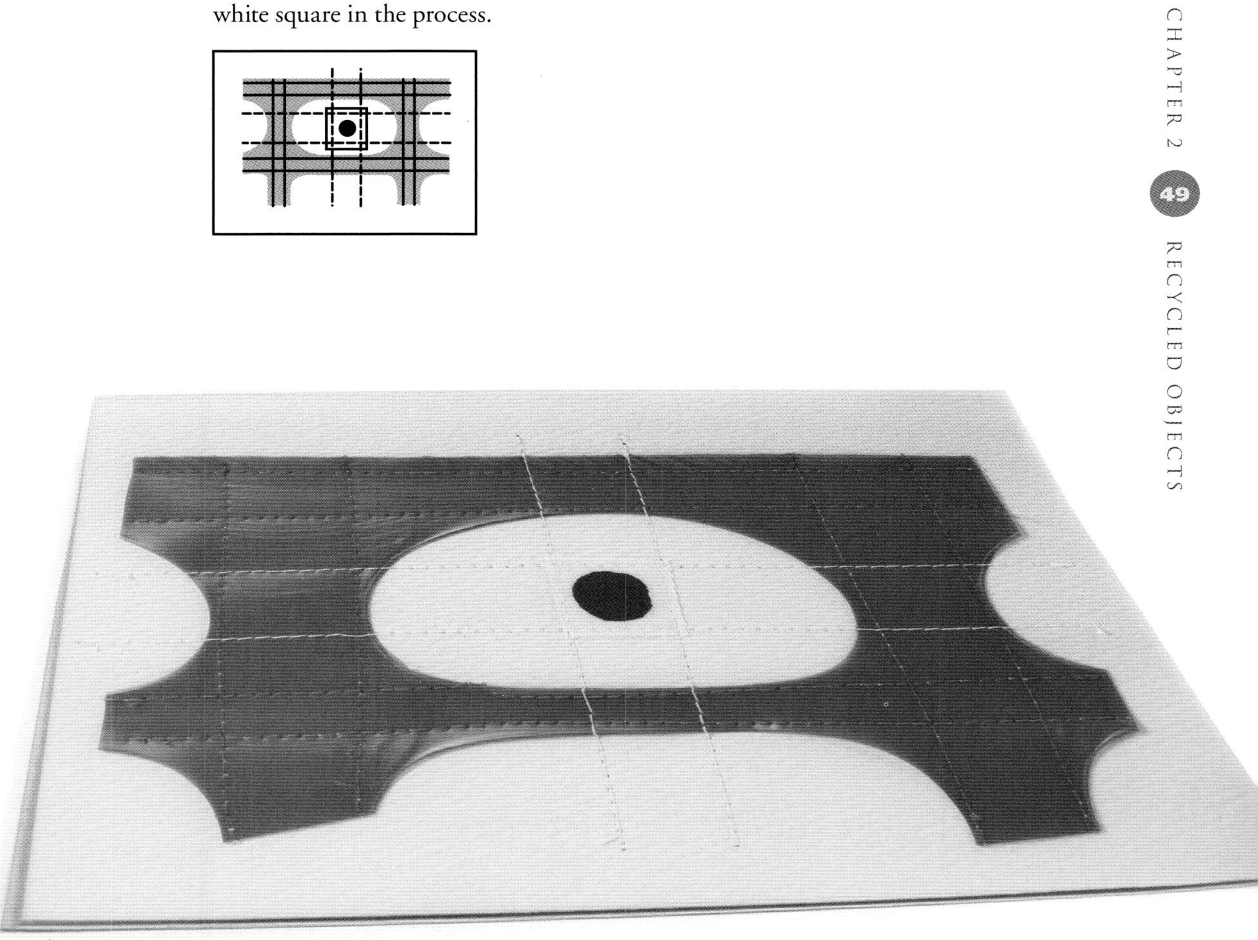

Herb Packet Card

After your next social or business event, reuse your name tag holder by filling it with herbs.

MATERIALS

- Square cream card stock, folded
- 1 tablespoon dried herbs (I used spearmint)
- 1 plastic name tag holder, about 4 1/4 x 3 5/8 inches (11 x 9 cm)
- Yellow-gold rickrack
- Yellow-gold thread, for sewing
- Cream thread, for bobbin

INSTRUCTIONS

1. Hold the card open and flat, face up.
2. Fill the name tag holder with dried herbs.
3. Place filled pouch on the center of the card front.

4. Lay a piece of rickrack across the top of the filled holder near the opening, with extra on each side of the pouch.

5. Stitch over the rickrack to attach it to the card and holder, stitching the top of the holder closed.

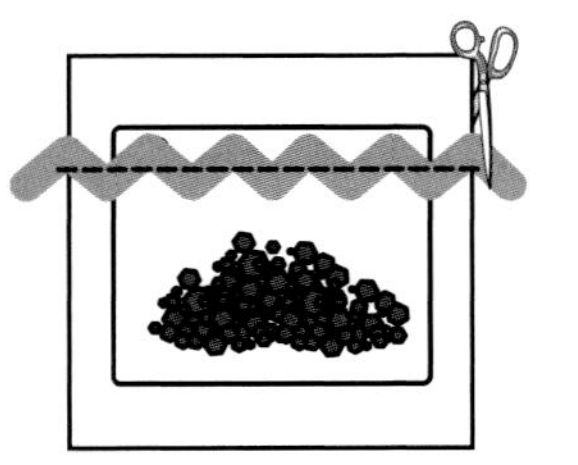

6. Using the sewing machine presser foot as a guide, stitch around all four edges of the name tag holder, to create a stitched box around it.

7. Trim the ends of any loose threads on the front and inside of the card.

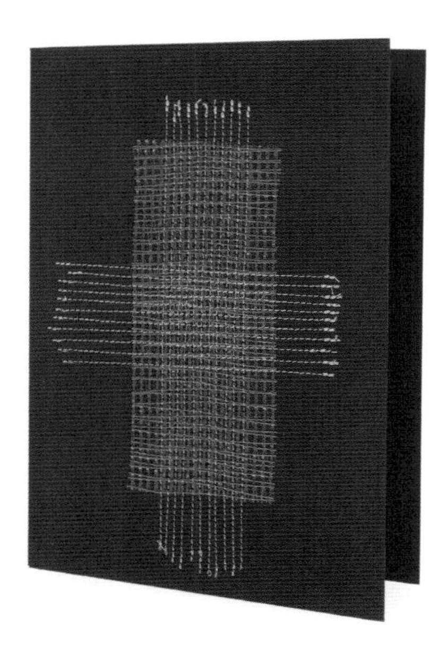

Winter Plaid

Create your own plaid pattern, using recycled netting and thread.

MATERIALS

- Rectangular portrait red card stock, folded
- 1 piece of flat green netting, from a bag of limes
- Yellow thread, for sewing
- Red thread, for bobbin

INSTRUCTIONS

1. Hold the card open and flat, face up.
2. Cut a piece of netting into a tall rectangle.
3. Place the rectangle piece of netting vertically in the center of the card front.

4. Stitch yellow lines vertically between the green net lines. Note: If you have trouble stitching between the green lines, use your presser foot as a guide for stitch placement instead.

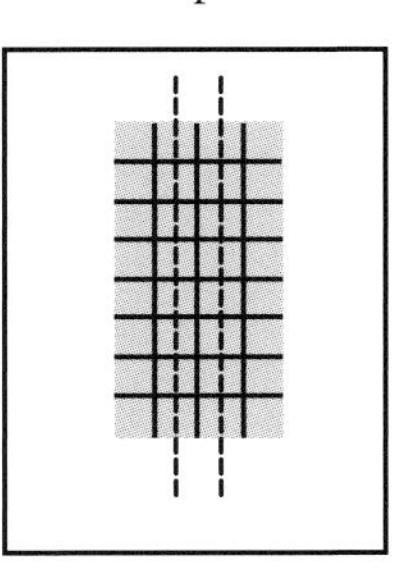

5. Stitch yellow lines horizontally between the green net lines.

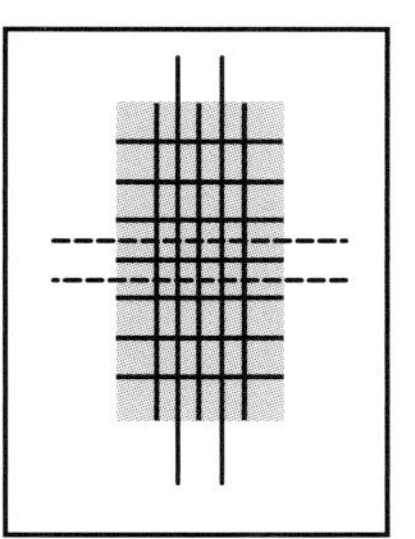

6. Trim the ends of any loose threads on the front and inside of the card.

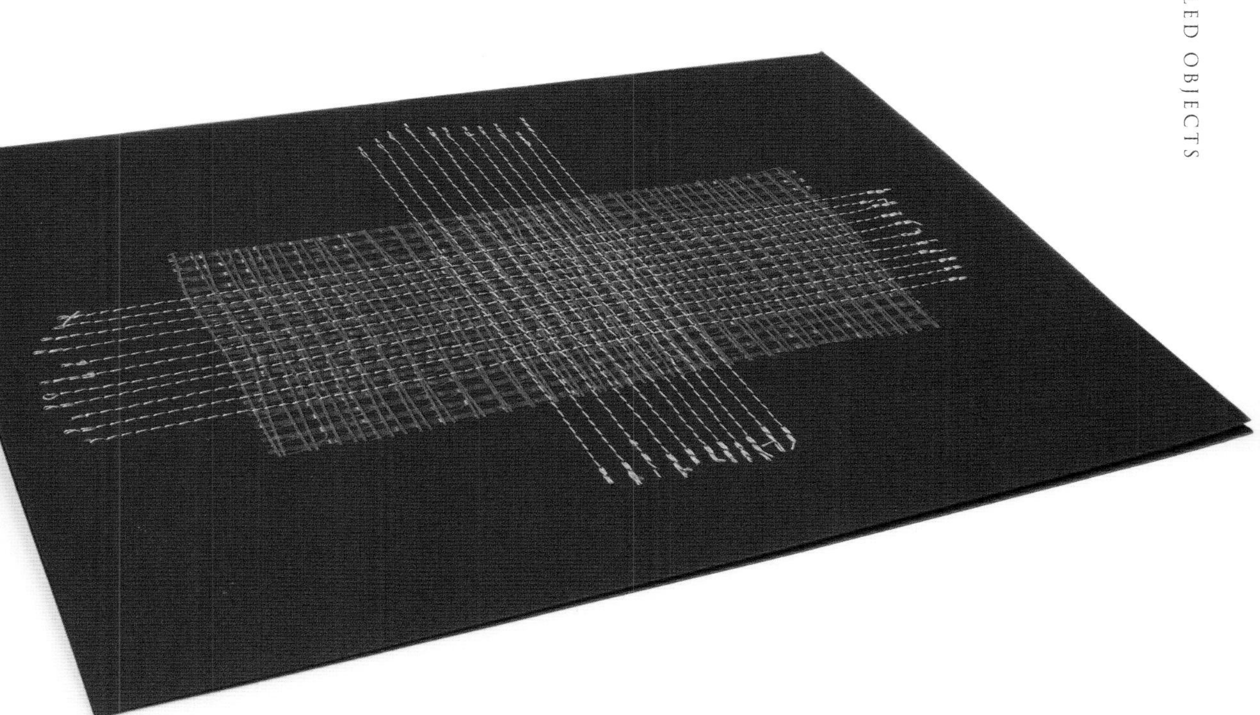

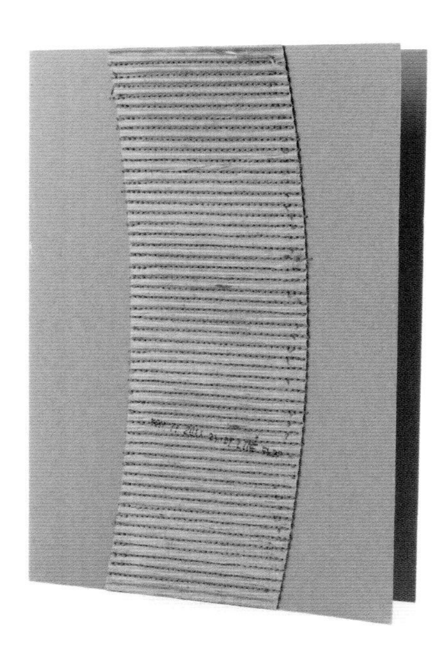

Coffee Cup Sleeve Recycled

The back of the coffee cup sleeve has an organic, tree trunk–like look.

MATERIALS

- Rectangular portrait green card stock, folded
- 1 coffee cup sleeve
- Green thread, for sewing and bobbin

INSTRUCTIONS

1. Hold the card open and flat, face up.
2. Open the coffee cup sleeve at the glued seam.
3. Center the opened coffee cup sleeve vertically on the card, corrugated side up.

4. Stitch inside the dents of the lines of the corrugated cardboard. Note: If you don't have the time or patience to stitch between each line, stitch every few lines or randomly.

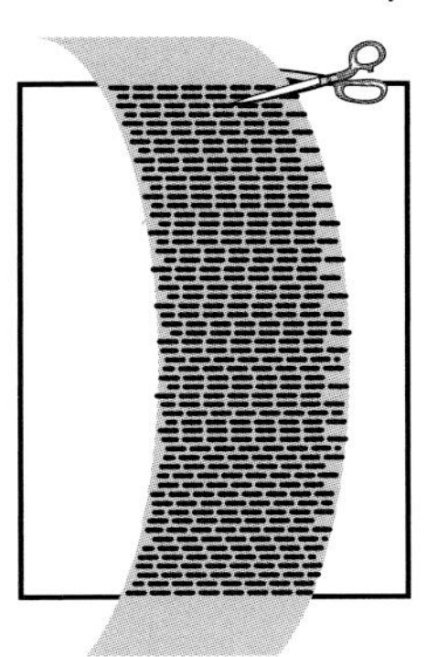

5. Cut off the parts of the sleeve that hang over the edge of the card.

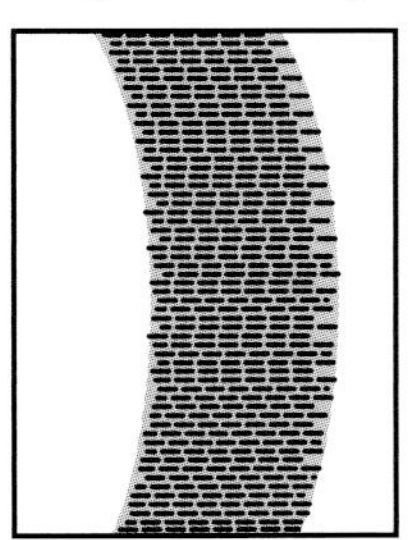

6. Trim the ends of any loose threads on the front and inside of the card.

Plastic Bag Strips

It's fun to cut used plastic bags into strips and use them creatively to make a design.

MATERIALS

- Square grape card stock, folded
- 1 thick plastic shopping bag with bright colors or patterns (I used a 344 bag; or substitute fabric or paper)
- Purple thread, for sewing and bobbin

INSTRUCTIONS

1. Hold the card open and flat, face up.
2. Trim the plastic bag into four strips that incorporate pattern or color. Discard the remainder of the bag.
3. Position and stitch the top of the first strip near the top of the card so the color or pattern is centered.

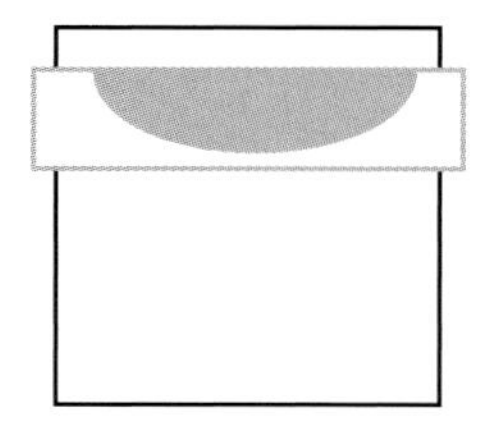

4. Position and stitch the next three strips, spacing them evenly apart.

5. Stitch the bottom of the last strip to the card.

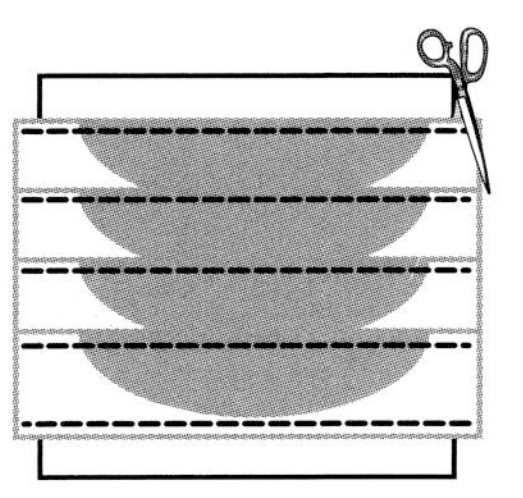

6. Trim the ends of the plastic strips that are hanging off the edges of the card.

7. Stitch around all four edges of the card, using your presser foot as a guide.

8. Trim the ends of any loose threads on the front and inside of the card.

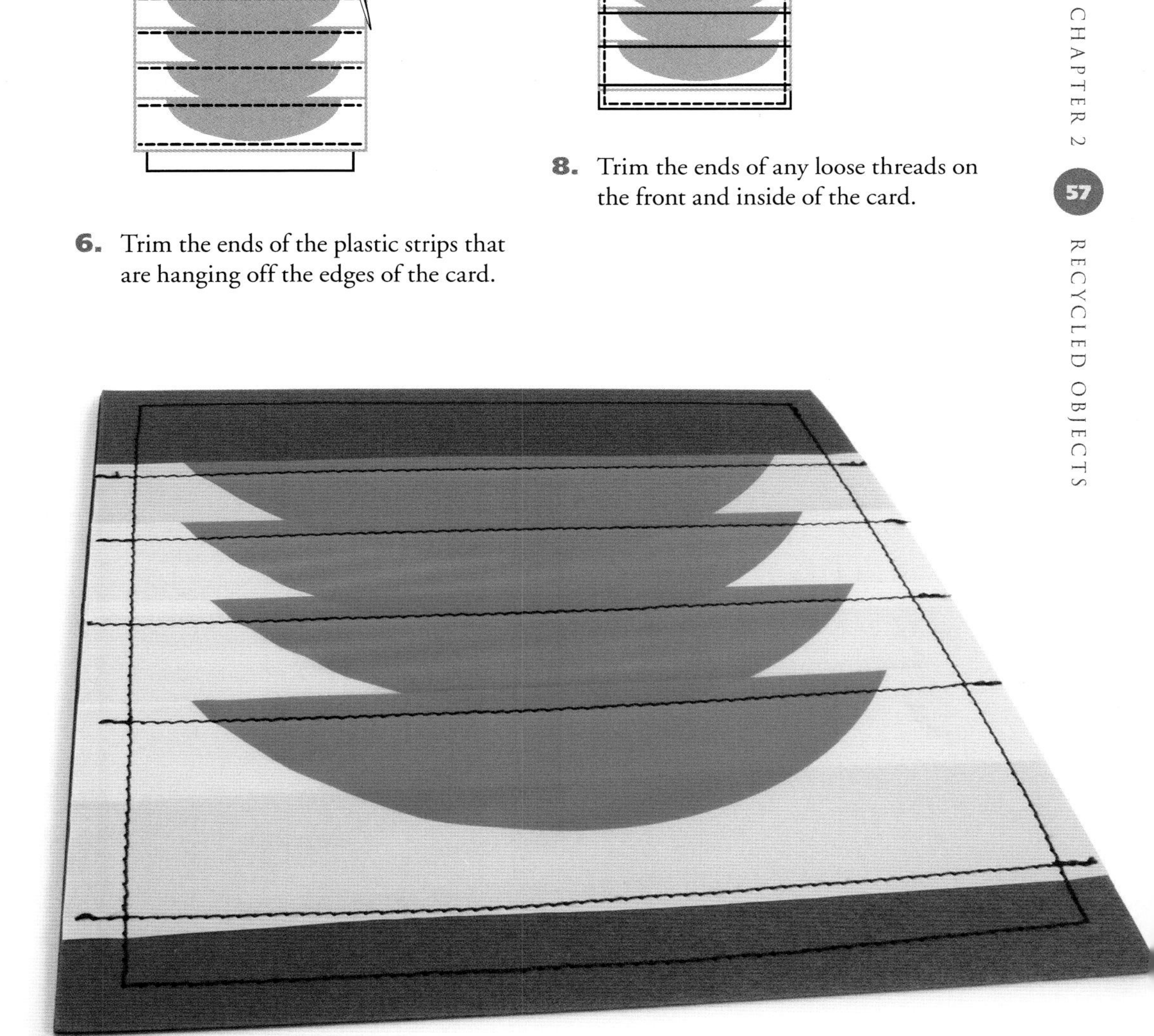

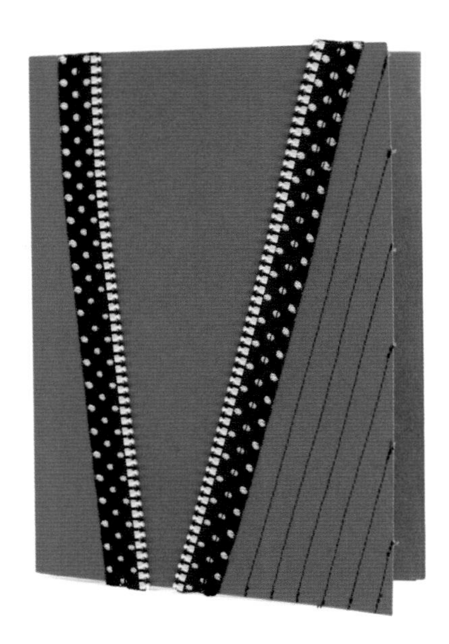

Zipped

This is a good way to use extra zippers that are in the sewing basket.

MATERIALS

- Rectangular portrait turquoise card stock, folded
- 1 (9-inch [23 cm]) or longer zipper
- Black thread, for sewing
- Turquoise thread, for bobbin

INSTRUCTIONS

1. Hold the card open and flat, face up.
2. Open the zipper and place on the card so it forms a V across the card, with the zipper pull off the card stock.

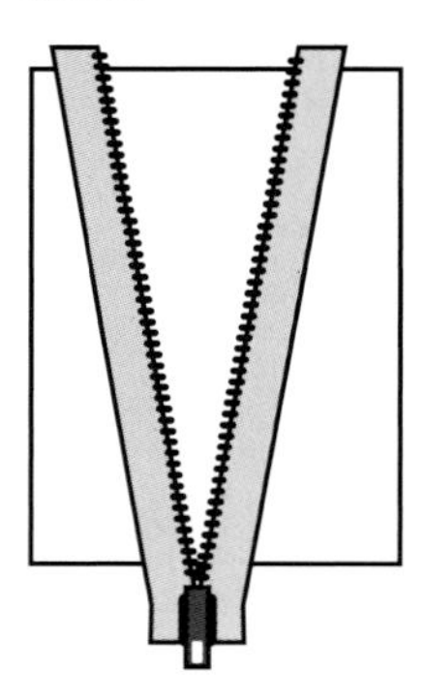

3. Stitch the opened zipper to the card. Optional: Stitch a second row closer to the zipper teeth.

4. Trim the overhanging zipper close to the edge of the card stock. Note: If it's not possible to cut through the zipper teeth, cut between the teeth, close to the edge.

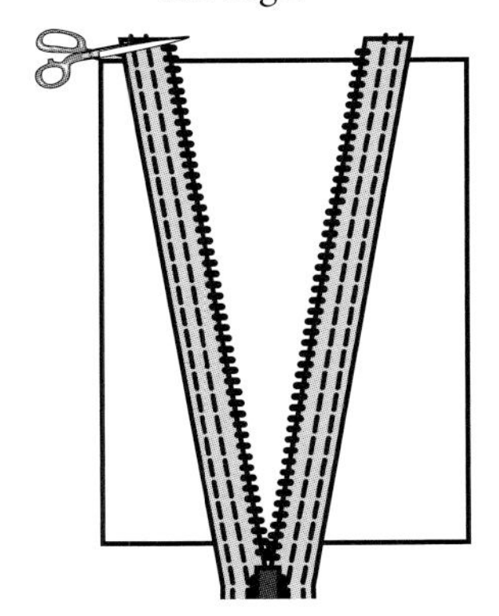

5. Using the presser foot of the sewing machine as a guide, sew additional lines to the right of the outside edge of the right-hand portion of zipper.

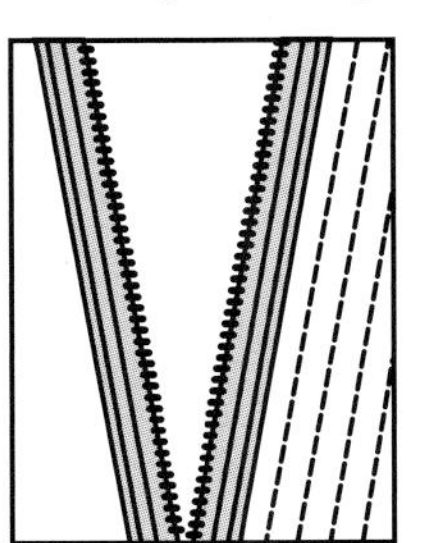

6. Repeat sewing additional lines to the right of the first line, until there is no more room on the card.

7. Trim the ends of any loose threads on the front and inside of the card.

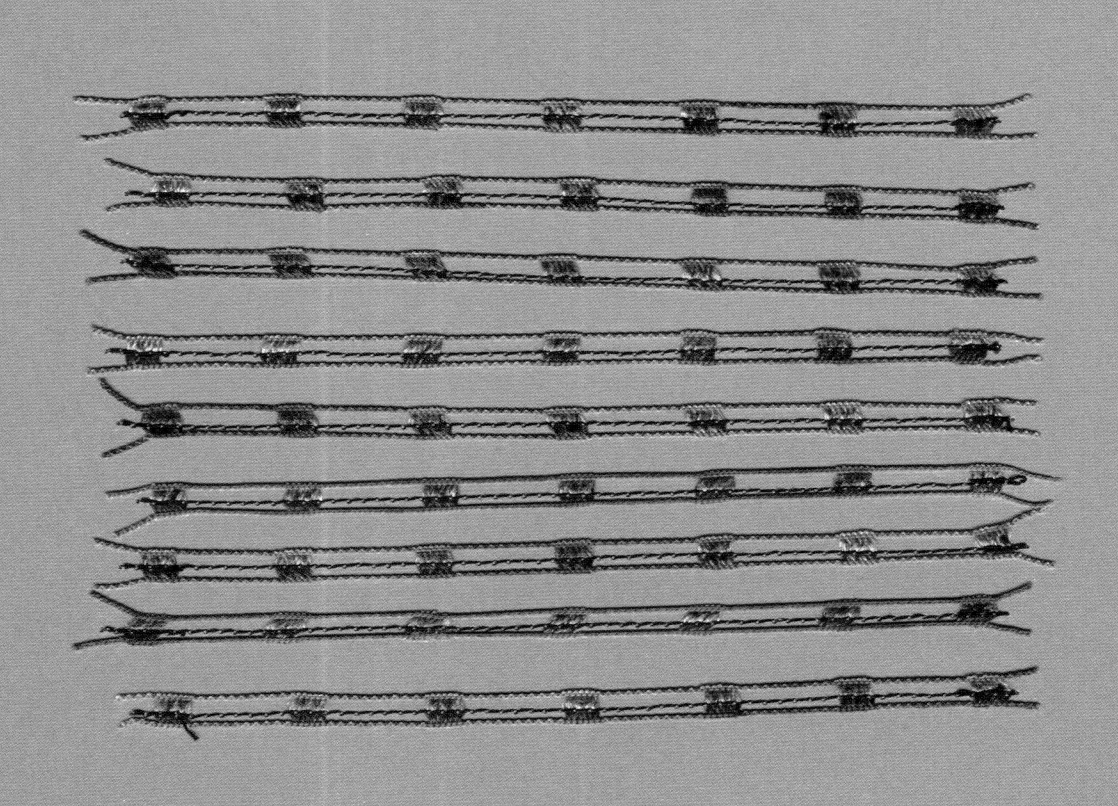

CHAPTER 3

Fabric and Paper

It's common to use different kinds of paper when designing cards. This chapter has some projects that use paper in a more traditional way, and in other projects, I push the boundaries further.

Clean cupcake and candy wrappers are fun to work with when circles are part of a design theme. You may want to consider using them instead of drawing and cutting out your own circles. These wrappers come in various colors, as well as in patterns such as stripes.

Sections of maps can be fun to use, when sharing a memory of a vacation or a weekend visit. To liven up the fact that I'm using a map, I like to match the colors of the highways to my thread color and extend the lines from the map onto the rest of the page, to create a secondary design.

In the kitchen, when cooking pasta, consider reusing the package of pasta that comes with the clear window to display the pasta shape. Cut around the window, leaving some surrounding paper from the package around all four sides, and place something special behind the window.

There are times when I've seen wrapped gifts in beautiful paper, with designs in a quality rivaling that of bed sheets or wallpaper. I've always felt it was a shame for the gift to be unwrapped and the paper thrown in the trash or recycle bin. Instead, consider cutting it up to reuse in card and other collage projects.

You may not have thought to use fabric as you would nice paper, but the uses of fabric are as unlimited as the colors and designs available. Cut out flowers, geometric patterns, stripes, and colors that inspire you from your stash, as well as pieces from old bedding or old clothes that you don't use anymore.

Similarly, consider using lace, whether from yardage, decoration, or used clothing. I especially like to use lace when creating sympathy cards, because it's more personal than a store-bought card.

Ribbon, as a sewing supply or taken from an unwrapped gift, can also be fun to use. Ribbon can be layered on top of other ribbons, woven, or tied in a bow and stitched to the card. Some ribbons are slippery, so consider stitching a sample to extra paper so you get a feel for how it is to work with when machine sewing.

Yarn and string are fun to use when decorating cards. They can be woven through fabric, such as eyelet lace, or couched (stitched) to fabric or the card itself, creating a textured line instead of using a marker.

It's very possible that you may not be able to find the exact materials that are used in these projects. Use the instructions as a guide, and tweak them as needed to create a card with your own materials.

Flower Power

If you aren't able to give someone flowers, you can brighten his or her day with a card that has flowers.

MATERIALS

- Square chartreuse card stock, folded
- 1 fabric flower, cut smaller than the actual card size (or substitute flower paper)
- White thread, for sewing and bobbin
- Optional: Green marker or green colored pencil

INSTRUCTIONS

1. Hold the card open and flat, face up.
2. Center the flower in the upper middle of the front of the card.
3. Using white thread, sew the flower in place slowly, using a zigzag stitch, stopping and turning the card as the edge of the flower turns.

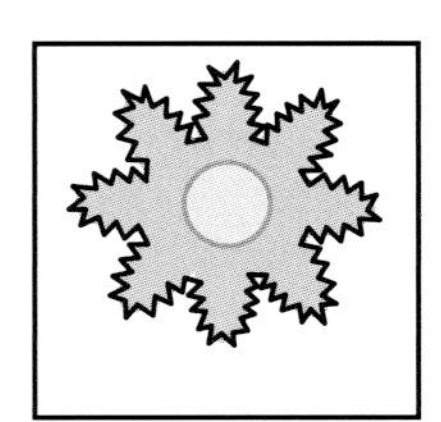

4. Using a straight stitch, sew two leaves, one at the bottom left of the flower and another at the right. Color in the leaves and stem, using a green marker or colored pencil, if you wish.

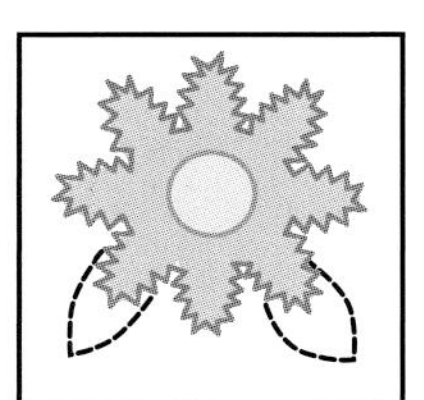

5. Trim the ends of any loose threads on the front and inside of the card.

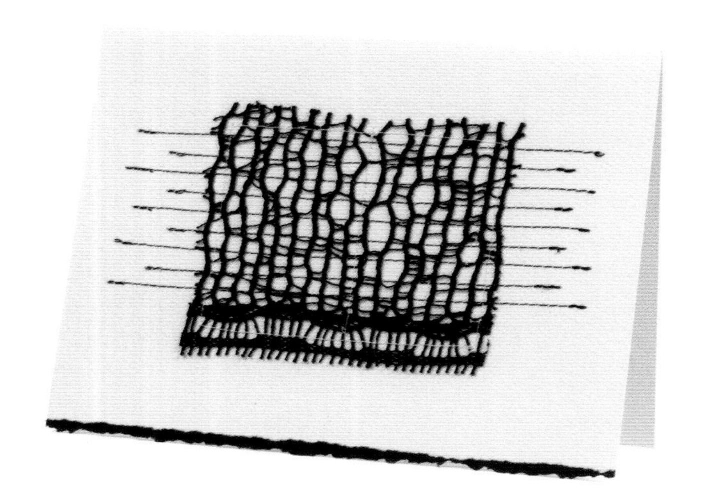

With Sympathies

A simple sympathy card made with black lace is a gentle visual way to express feelings of loss.

MATERIALS

- Rectangular landscape off-white card stock with a black ragged edge, folded
- 1 piece of black lace, cut smaller than the size of the card
- White thread, for sewing
- Black thread, for sewing
- Off-white thread, for bobbin
- Optional: Black marker, if your card stock doesn't have a black edge

INSTRUCTIONS

1. Hold the card open and flat, face up.
2. Center a black piece of lace on the card front.
3. Using white thread, sew straight stitches top to bottom in the center and close to the inside edges of the lace to keep it in place.

4. With black thread, sew a straight stitch, starting about an inch (2.5 cm) away from one side of the lace, over the top of it, and past it by about an inch (2.5 cm).

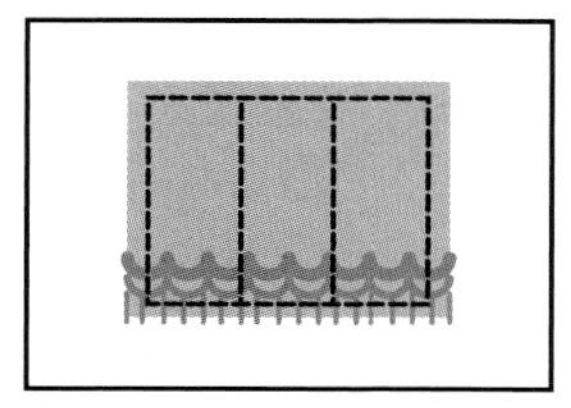

5. Using the presser foot of the sewing machine as a guide, sew additional lines to the right of the first line, until the right side is attached to the card. The beginning and end of each line can vary from line to line.

6. Repeat sewing additional lines to the right of the previous line, until most of the lace is covered with lines of stitches.

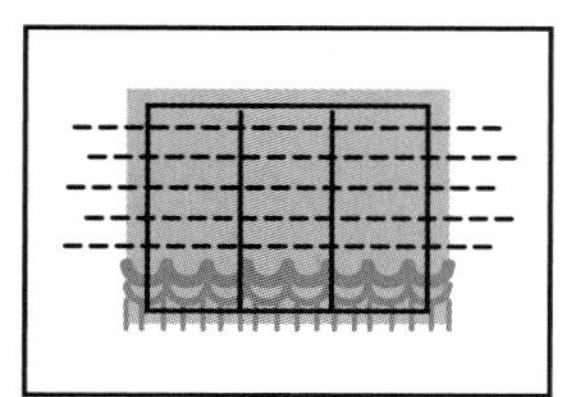

7. Trim the ends of any loose threads on the front and inside of the card.

OPTIONAL: *Color the bottom edge of the card front using a black marker, if the card stock doesn't have a black edge at the bottom.*

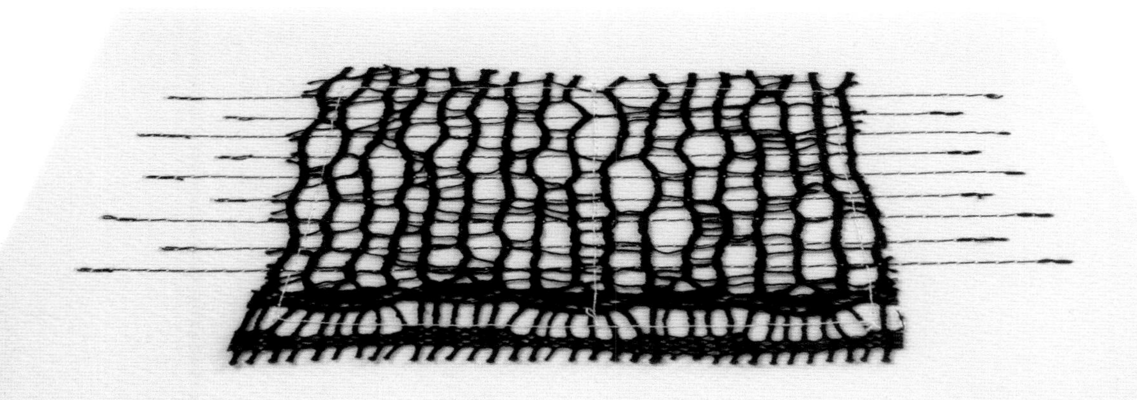

The Gift Box

Sew a ribbon on the card and use it as a way to present cash or gift certificates.

MATERIALS

- Rectangular landscape green card stock, folded
- 1 length of blue ribbon, at least 24 inches (61 cm) long
- Blue thread, for sewing
- Green thread, for sewing and bobbin

INSTRUCTIONS

1. Hold the card open and flat, face up.
2. Take both ends of the ribbon and tie a knot, being sure to leave 2 to 3 inches (5 to 7.5 cm) of excess. Trim the ribbon ends on the diagonal.
3. Place the knotted section of the ribbon on a flat surface. Using the knot as the center of your measurement, cut the ribbon to be at least 2 inches (5 cm) longer than the width of your card, and cut another piece of ribbon 2 inches (5 cm) longer than the height. This will allow for overhang as you work.
4. Place the second piece of ribbon flat, centered vertically on the card. Stitch small zigzag stitches to attach the ribbon to the card, using blue thread.

5. Place the knotted piece of ribbon horizontally centered on the card, over the vertical piece of ribbon, at right angles. Center the knot over the stitched ribbon. Stitch small blue zigzag stitches over the knotted ribbon, stopping before the knotted section.

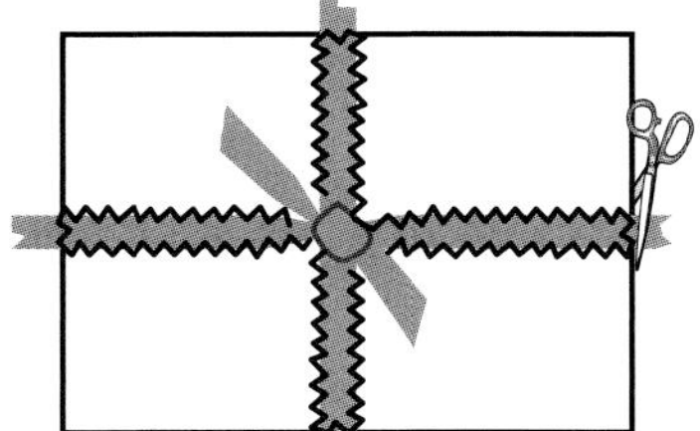

6. Stitch all the ends of the ribbon where they meet the edges of the card, and trim close to the edges.

7. Using the presser foot of the sewing machine as a guide, sew a green line of straight stitches near the top folded

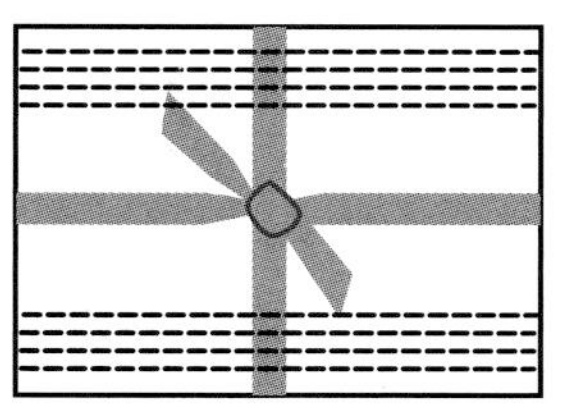

edge of the card. Repeat so there are a total of four lines at the top, and four lines at the bottom edge of the card.

8. Using the presser foot as a guide, sew six vertical rows of green straight stitches on the right and left sides of the card.

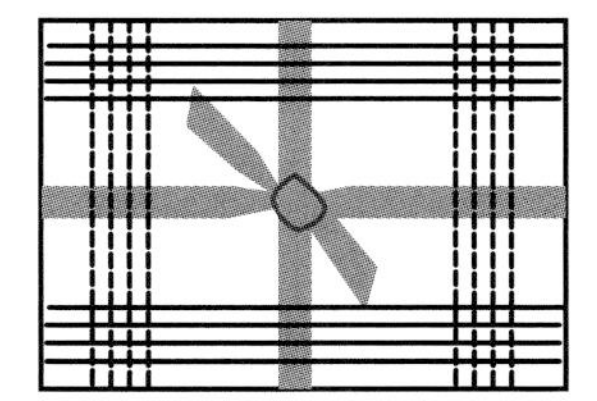

9. Trim the ends of any loose threads on the front and inside of the card.

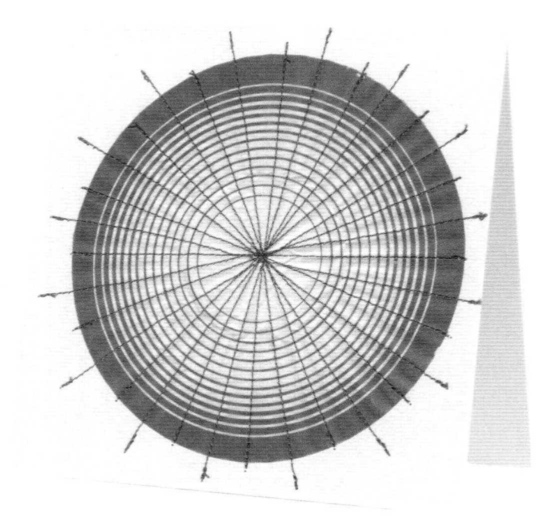

Stitched Starburst

Create a starburst card, using a cupcake wrapper and thread.

MATERIALS

- Square white card stock, folded
- 1 large striped or patterned cupcake wrapper (or substitute a solid color)
- Orange thread, for sewing
- Green thread, for sewing
- White thread, for bobbin

INSTRUCTIONS

1. Hold the card open and flat, face up.
2. Use your fingers to press open the pleats of the cupcake wrapper on a hard surface.
3. Center the cupcake wrapper in the center of the card front.
4. Holding the wrapper as flat as possible, sew straight stitches, using orange thread, from near the outside edge of the wrapper and across the center, ending near the outside of the edge on the other side.

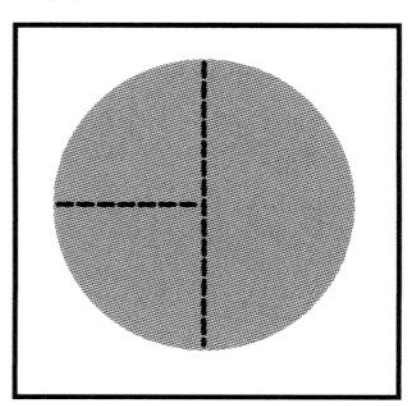

5. Starting at the center of the wrapper, rotate the card and stitch 90 degrees from the first line, ending at the outer edge. Rotate the card and start again in the center, continuing the previous line 90 degrees from the first line, ending at the edge of the wrapper.

6. Repeat stitching from one end of the wrapper to the other end, sewing through the middle of the quarters and again through the middle of the eighths, so there are stitched lines resembling the hours of a clock.

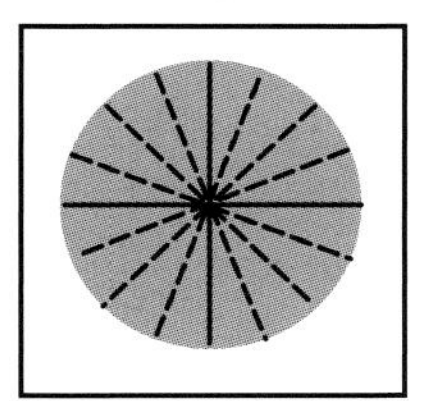

7. Change the thread color to green and stitch straight lines between each of the orange lines, starting outside of the edge of the wrapper and ending outside at the end.

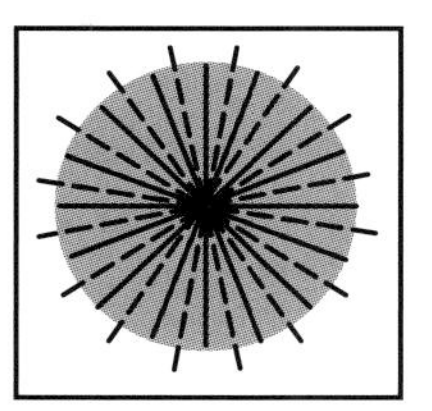

8. Trim the ends of any loose threads on the front and inside of the card.

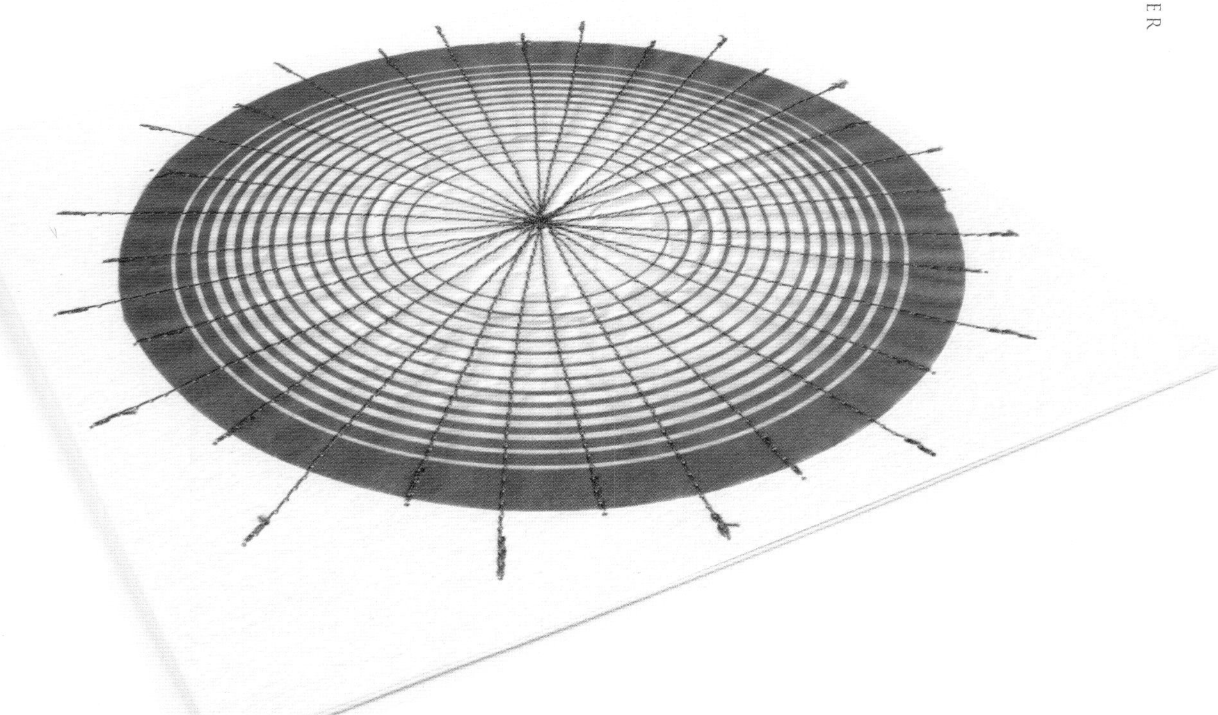

Cluny Lace Stripes

Stripes of off-white lace on black offer a nice positive-negative geometric effect.

MATERIALS

- Rectangular landscape black card stock, folded
- 1 (27-inch [69 cm]) length of Cluny lace or similar lace trimming, cut into three 9-inch (23 cm) lengths
- Off-white thread, for sewing
- Black thread, for bobbin

INSTRUCTIONS

1. Hold the card open and flat, face up.
2. Place one piece of lace centered across the card front, and stitch near the top of the lace.
3. Place the next length of lace below the first piece and stitch in place.
4. Place the last length of lace above the first piece and stitch.

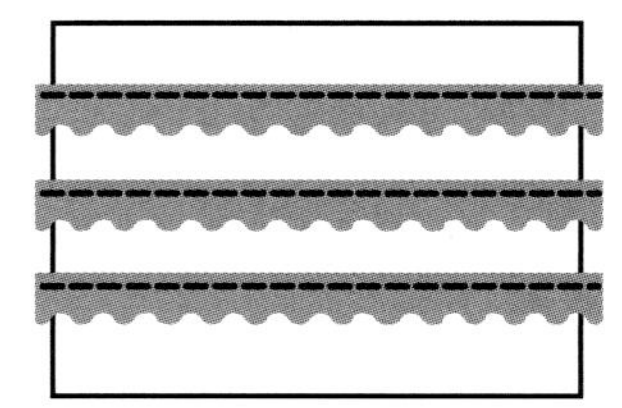

5. Stitch around all four edges of the card, using your presser foot as a guide. Note: Sew slowly when stitching over the lace, being careful to keep it flat on the card stock.

6. Stitch again inside the stitches from the previous step, centering the stitches between the stitches and the edges of the card. Note: Sew slowly when stitching over the lace.

7. Trim the edges of lace hanging off the card.

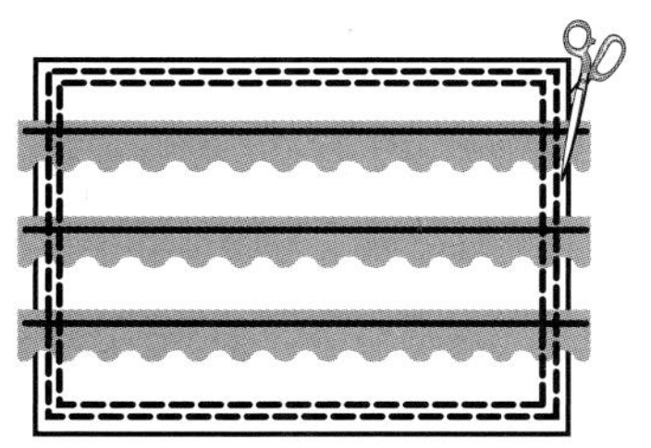

8. Trim the ends of any loose threads on the front and inside of the card.

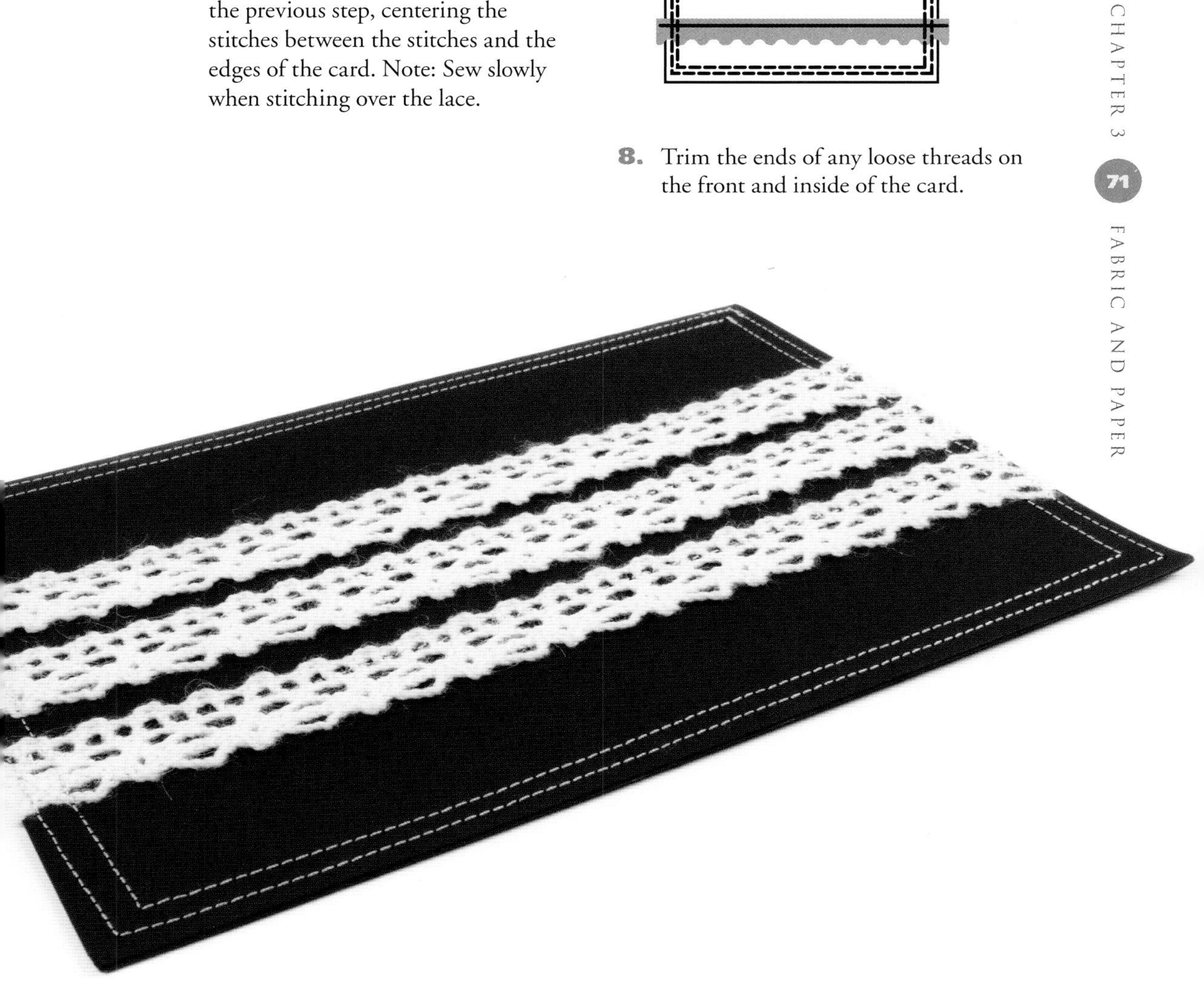

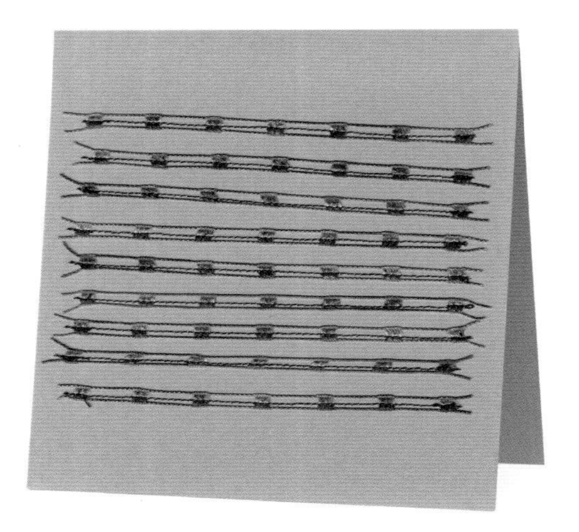

Stripes of Yarn

Horizontal stripes of yarn create a colorful vertical stripe.

MATERIALS

- Square lilac card stock, folded
- 9 pieces of decorative yarn, each just shorter than the width of the card
- Black thread, for sewing
- Lilac thread, for bobbin

INSTRUCTIONS

1. Hold the card open and flat, face up.
2. Place one piece of yarn centered in the middle of the card front and stitch. NOTE: *Sew slowly if the yarn is slippery or moves around.*

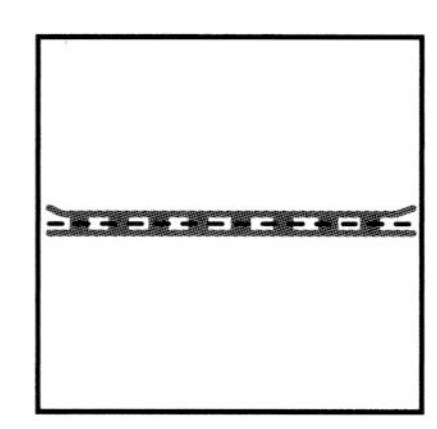

3. Place the next four lengths of yarn below the first piece and stitch into place.

4. Place the four more lengths of yarn above the first piece and stitch.

5. Trim the ends of any loose threads on the front and inside of the card.

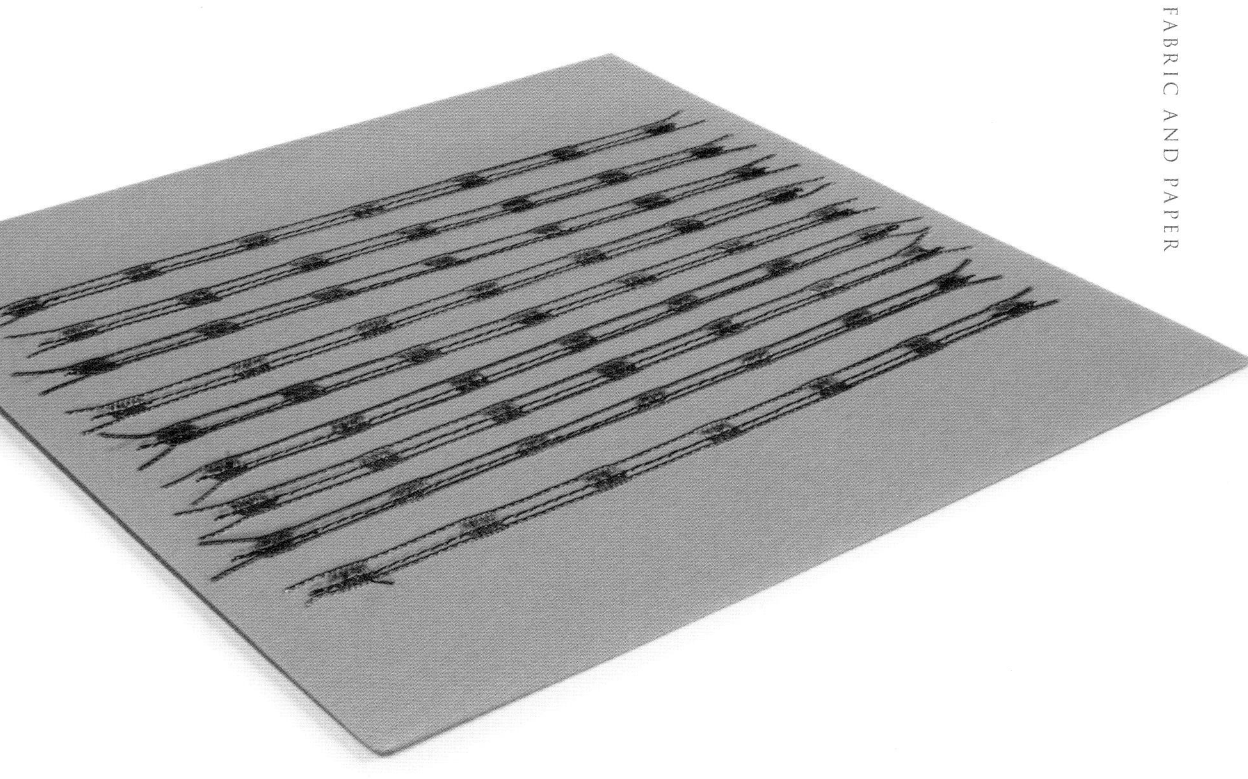

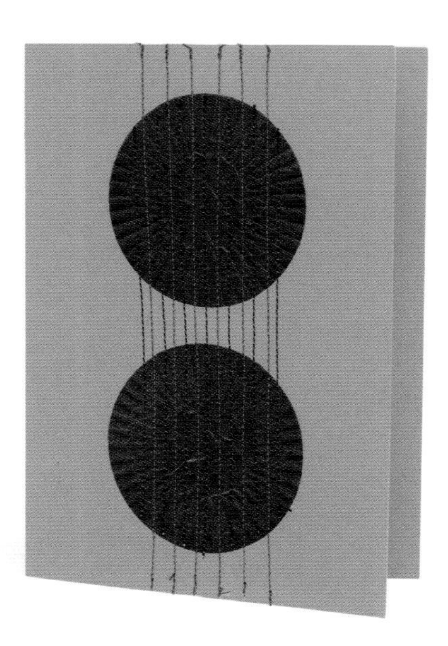

Two Brown Dots

Recycle the wrappers from a box of chocolates to keep the sweet memory.

MATERIALS

- Rectangular portrait kraft brown card stock, folded
- 2 clean brown wrappers from a box of chocolates
- Black thread, for sewing
- Orange thread, for sewing
- Khaki brown thread, for bobbin

INSTRUCTIONS

1. Hold the card open and flat, face up.
2. Use your fingers to press open the pleats of the candy wrappers on a hard surface.
3. Center two candy wrappers vertically in the center of the card, one above the other, with a little space between them.
4. Holding the wrappers as flat as possible, sew a line of black straight stitches, starting at the center top of the outside edge of the top wrapper, continuing over the card, and ending at the bottom edge of the bottom wrapper.

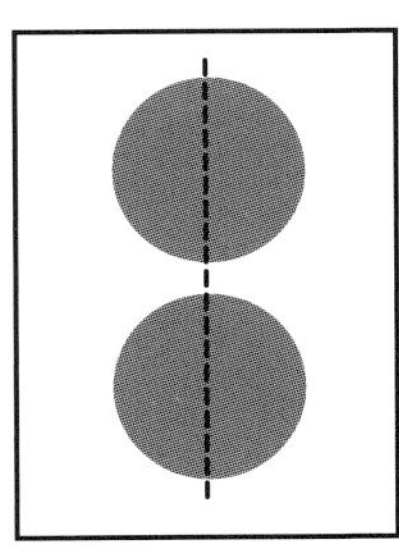

5. Using the sewing machine presser foot as a guide, stitch three lines to the left side and then to the right side of the first sewn line, starting and stopping at the top and bottom edges of the wrapper.

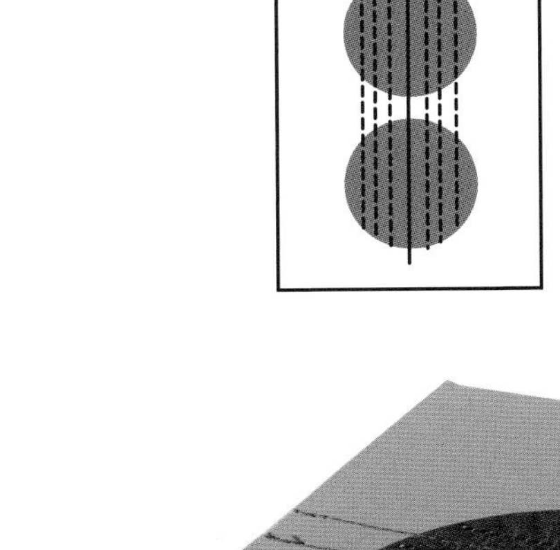

6. Using orange thread, stitch between each of the black lines of stitches, starting at the top of the card and ending at the bottom edge.

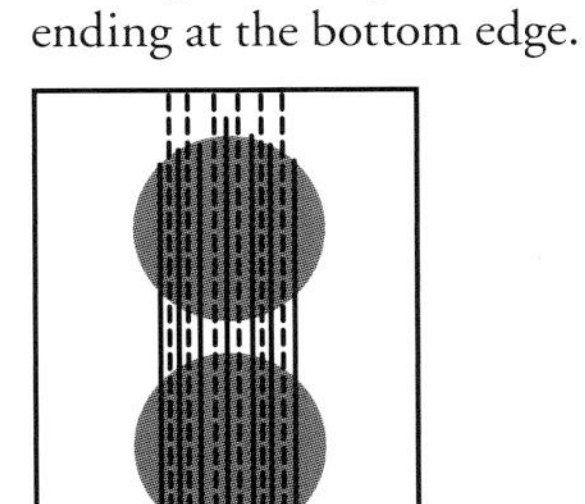

7. Trim the ends of any loose threads on the front and inside of the card.

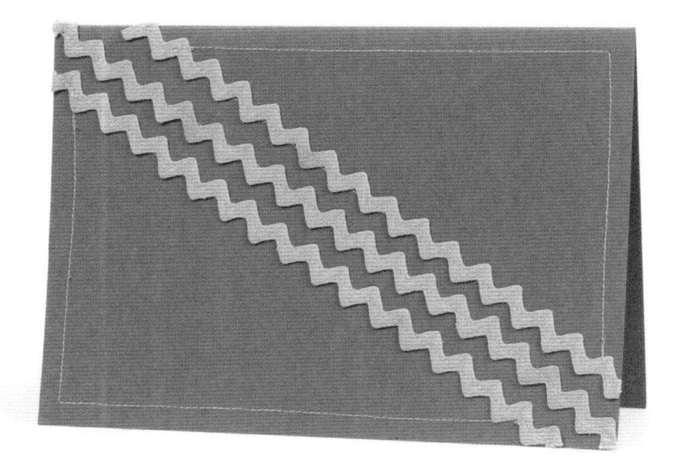

Rickrack Stripes

Rickrack, which was very commonly used in the 1950s and '60s, is now becoming retro cool.

MATERIALS

- Rectangular landscape peacock blue card stock, folded
- 3 pieces yellow rickrack, each more than 9 inches (23 cm) long
- Yellow thread, for sewing
- Peacock blue thread, for bobbin

INSTRUCTIONS

1. Hold the card open and flat, face up.
2. Stitch one piece of rickrack diagonally across the front of the card, using yellow thread, from the upper left to the lower right corners.

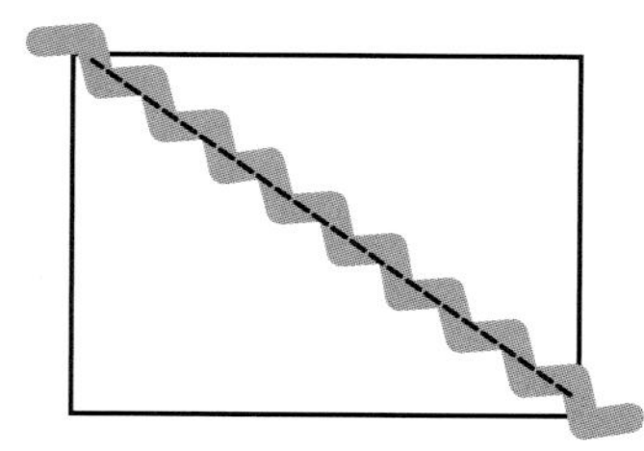

3. Stitch the second and third pieces of rickrack slightly above and below the first piece.
4. Trim the edges of the rickrack hanging off the edge of the card.

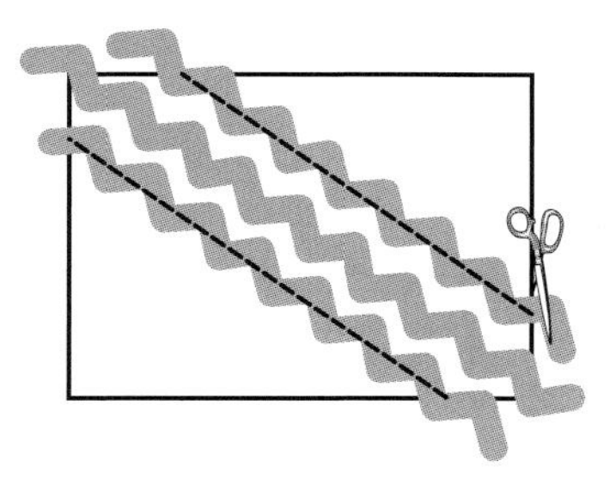

5. Using the sewing machine presser foot as a guide, stitch starting from the rickrack in the upper left corner, across the top, and down the right side.

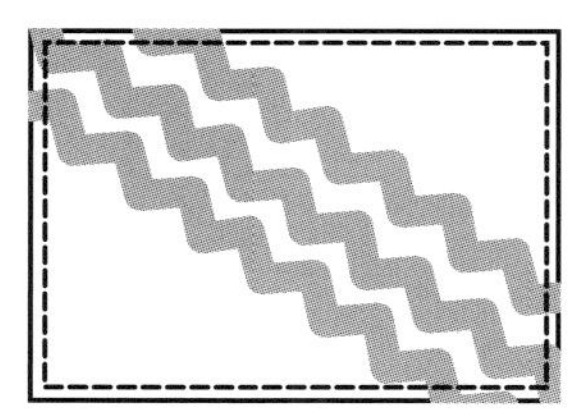

6. Stitch again from the bottom right corner across the bottom and up to the rickrack on the upper left side.
7. Trim the ends of any loose threads on the front and inside of the card.

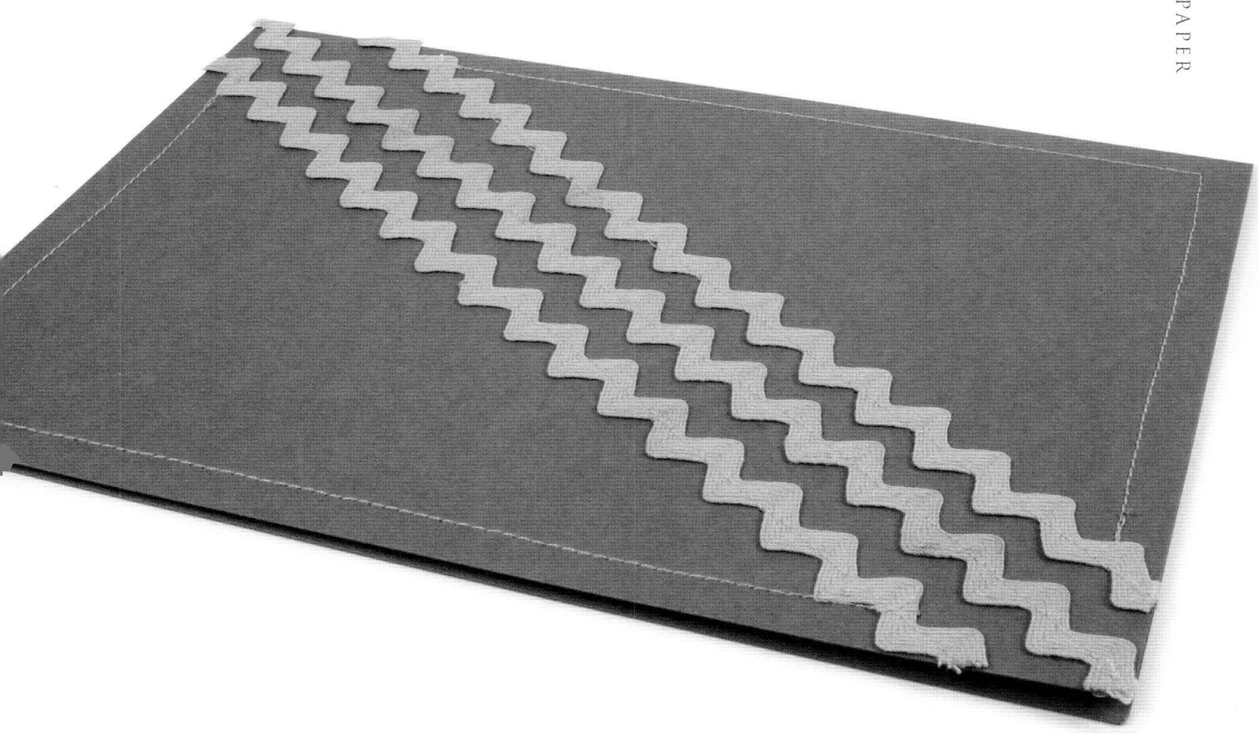

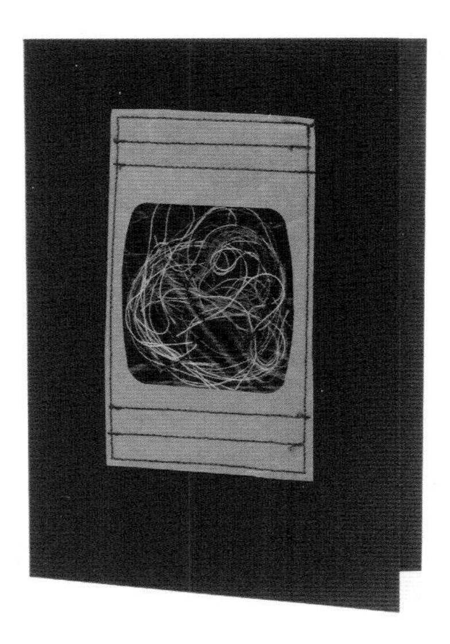

Window of Opportunity

The clear window found on some containers of pasta offers a design opportunity after the pasta is put to good use in the kitchen.

MATERIALS

- Rectangular portrait red card stock, folded
- 1 (1-pound [454 g]) paper pasta bag (or box) with a clear window as part of the packaging
- Thread trimmings, from other projects in this book or from other sewing projects
- Red thread, for sewing and bobbin

INSTRUCTIONS

1. Hold the card open and flat, face up.
2. Cut around the clear window on the pasta bag, leaving as much paper around it as possible above and below, without any printed text on the paper.

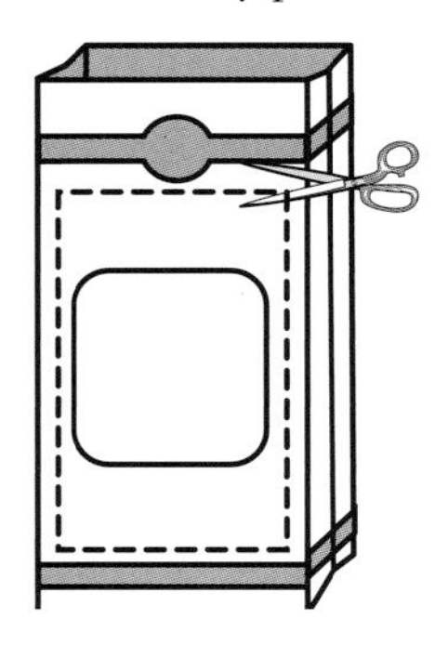

3. Place the paper pasta bag window centered on the card front.
4. Select sections of colored threads and place them behind the clear window from the bag.
5. Stitch near the outer edge of all four sides of the paper window, attaching it to the card.

6. Using the presser foot of the sewing machine as a guide, sew two additional lines on the paper, above and below the window.

7. Trim the ends of any loose threads on the front and inside of the card.

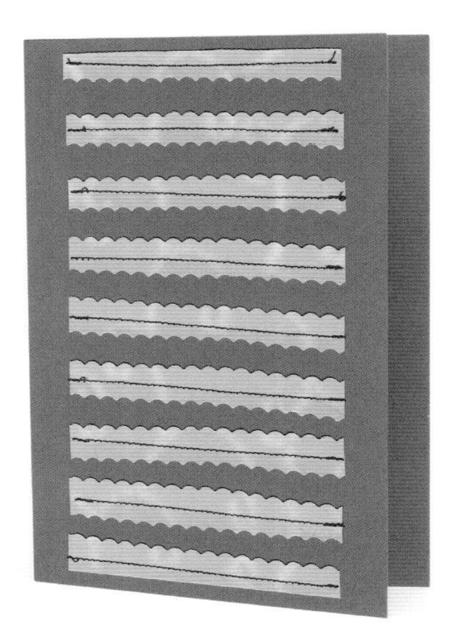

Scalloped Stripes

Pinking shear–like scissors come with different shapes, including scallop patterns.

MATERIALS

- Rectangular portrait grape card stock, folded
- 1 (3 3/4 x 3 3/4-inch [9.5 x 9.5 cm]) piece of textured paper (I used green)
- Pair of scallop-edged scissors
- Purple thread, for sewing and bobbin

INSTRUCTIONS

1. Hold the card open and flat, face up.
2. Trim the textured paper into nine thin strips, using scalloped scissors.

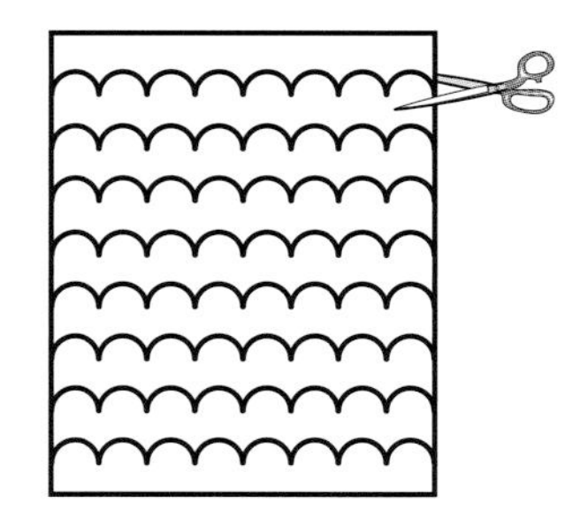

3. Position and stitch the top of the first strip centered near the top of the card.

4. Position and stitch the centered bottom strip, then the middle one, spacing it in the middle center of the card.

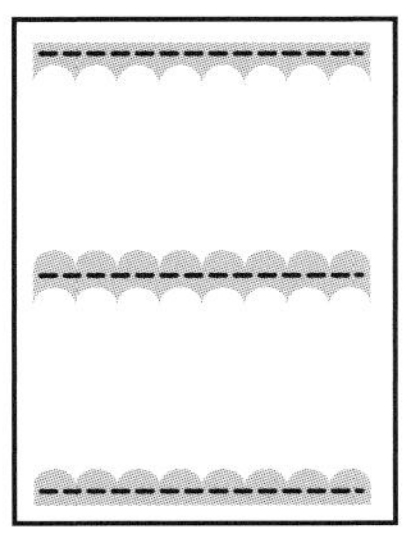

5. Stitch three strips at the upper section of the card, and three more in the bottom section.

6. Trim the edges of any loose threads on the front and inside of the card.

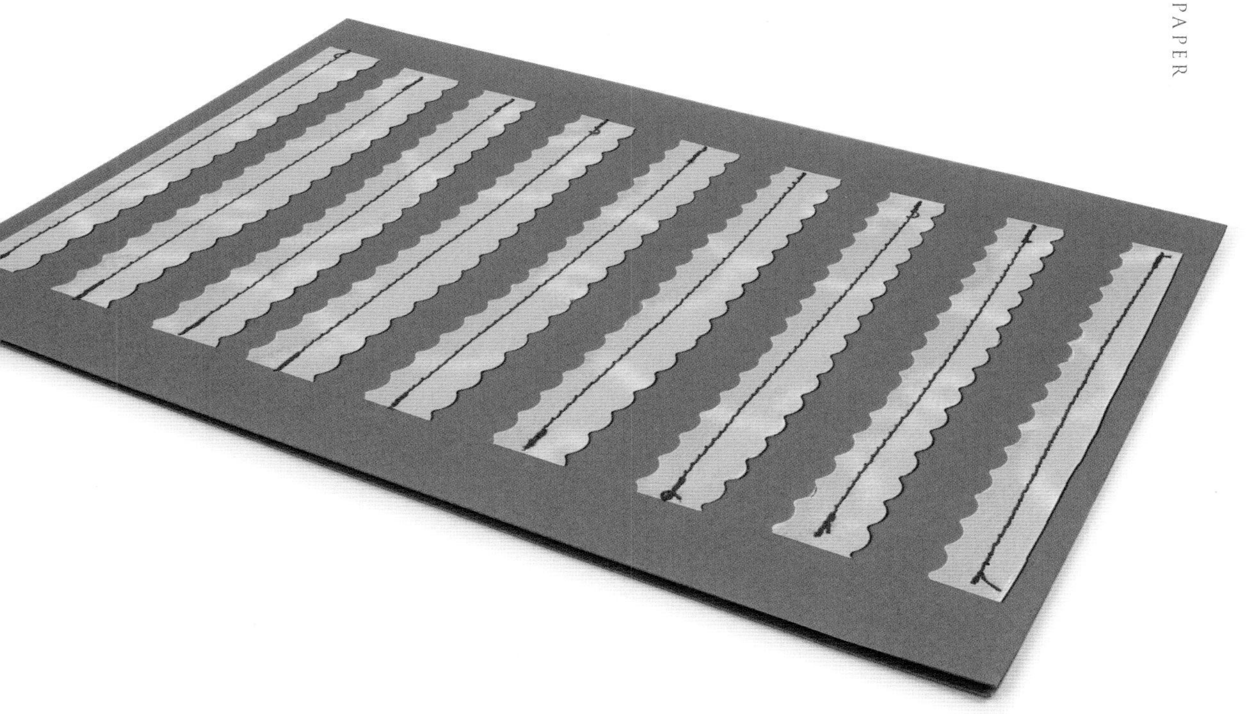

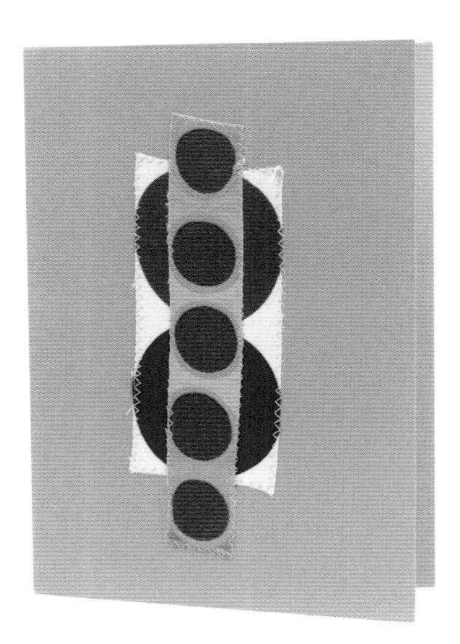

Circles on Circles

Overlap a strip of small fabric circles over a strip of larger circles, to create a new design.

MATERIALS

- Rectangular portrait gray card stock, folded
- 1 piece of fabric with five small circles in a row. The fabric should be shorter than the height of the card.
- 1 piece of fabric with two large circles in a row. This piece should be shorter and wider than the fabric with five small circles.
- Gray thread, for sewing and bobbin

INSTRUCTIONS

1. Hold the card open and flat, face up.
2. Center the piece of fabric with the large circles on the card front. Stitch with zigzag stitches to attach to the card. Note: Sew slowly and hold the fabric in place if it slides as you sew.

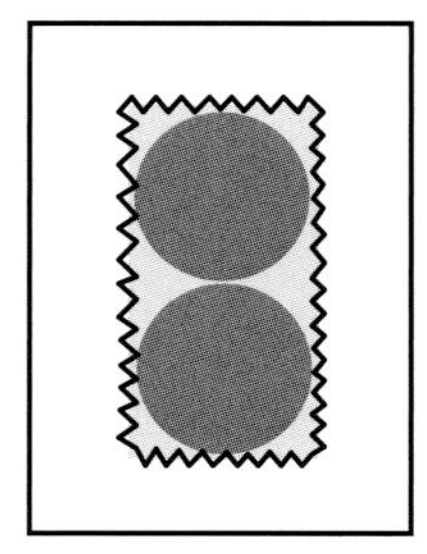

3. Center the piece of fabric with five small colored circles over the two large colored fabric circles. Stitch with zigzag stitches.

4. Trim the ends of any loose threads on the front and inside of the card.

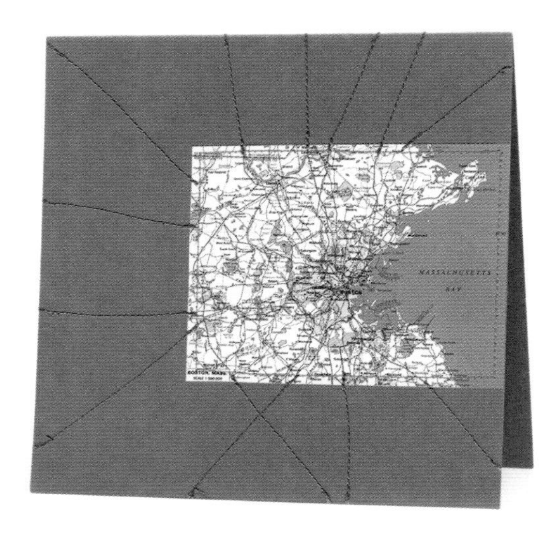

Map Detail Design

The highways on a road map always look similar to a spider web.

MATERIALS

- Square peacock blue card stock, folded
- 1 section of a paper map, about 2 $\frac{3}{4}$ x 3 $\frac{5}{8}$ inches (7 x 9 cm)
- Peacock blue thread, for sewing and bobbin
- Pink thread, for sewing (or choose other colors to match highway lines)

INSTRUCTIONS

1. Hold the card open and flat, face up.
2. Trim the edges of a paper map so it is smaller than the size of the card.
3. Position and stitch the map to the right edge of the card, using peacock blue thread. Note: Place the map elsewhere on the card to represent a different body of water, or to show surrounding land.

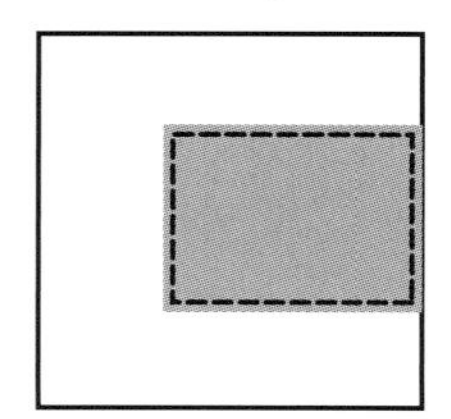

4. Stitch highway lines from the edge of the paper map out onto the card front, to create a design of sewn lines that end at the card edge or at the fold.

5. Trim the edges of any loose threads on the front and inside of the card.

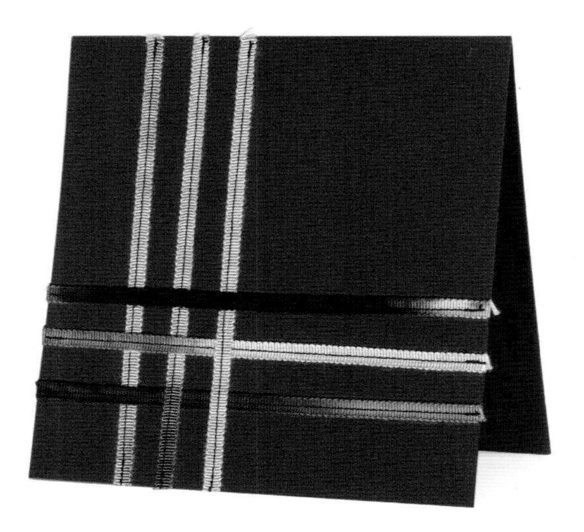

Faux Woven Ribbon

Create the appearance of woven ribbon on the card.

MATERIALS

- Square red card stock, folded
- 1 1/2 yards (115 cm) of 1/4-inch-wide (6-mm-wide) ribbon cut into 6 (9-inch [23 cm]) lengths
- Black thread, for sewing
- Red thread, for bobbin

INSTRUCTIONS

1. Hold the card open and flat, face up.
2. Position and stitch one length of ribbon vertically, 1 inch (2.5 cm) from the left side of the card. Note: If the ribbon is slippery on the card, stitch slowly as you hold it in place.

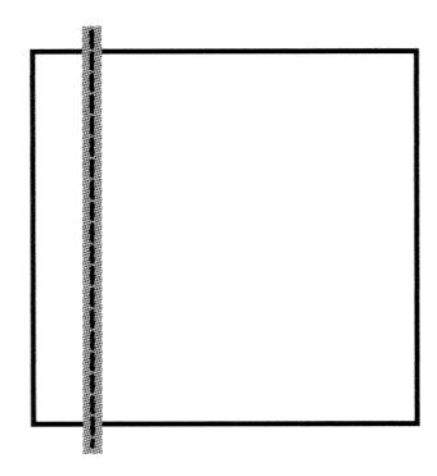

3. Position and stitch another length of ribbon horizontally, 1 inch (2.5 cm) from the bottom.

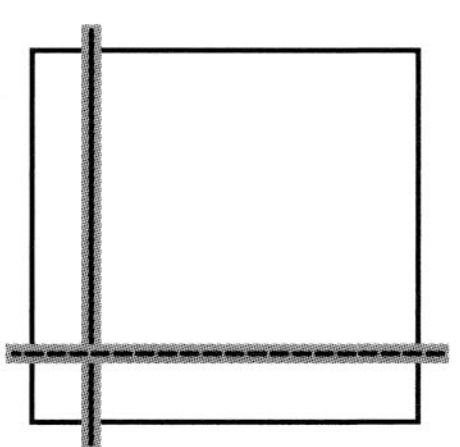

4. Alternate positioning and stitching the additional lengths of ribbon, horizontally and then vertically, spacing them slightly away from the other.

5. Trim the ribbon hanging off the card, to the card edge.

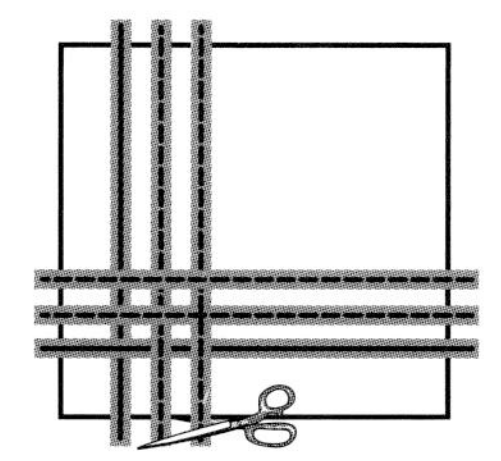

6. Trim the ends of any loose threads on the front and inside of the card.

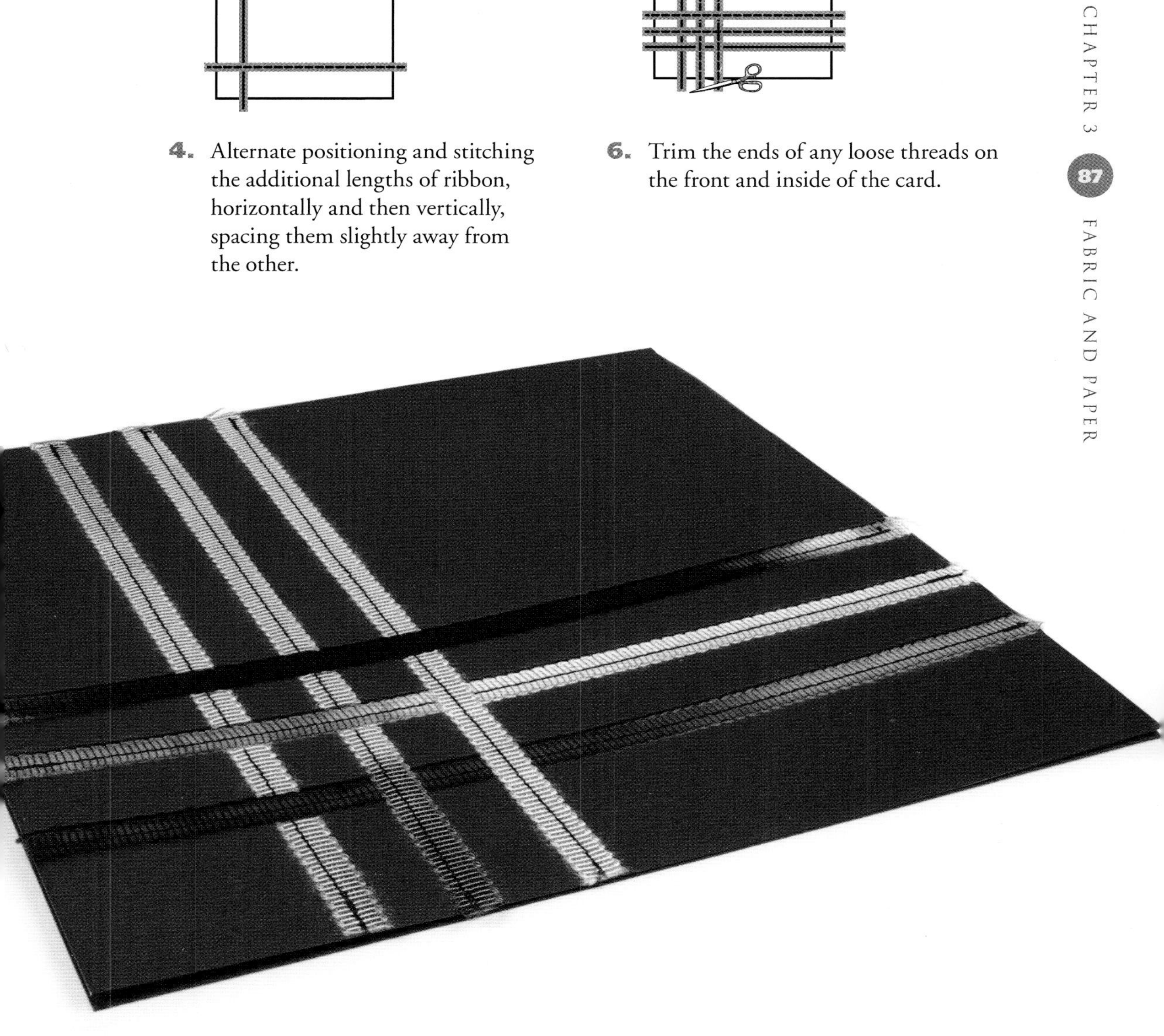

Recycled Images

Don't hesitate to reuse commercial paper if your drawing skills are shaky.

MATERIALS

- Rectangular landscape blue card stock, folded
- 1 image cut from wrapping paper (or substitute images from used cards or magazines)
- Blue thread, for sewing and bobbin
- Red thread, for sewing

INSTRUCTIONS

1. Hold the card open and flat, face up.
2. Place the image centered on the card front, and stitch close to the edge to attach using blue thread.
3. Using the sewing machine presser foot as a guide, stitch a red straight line, using the bottom edge of the card as your guide.

4. Stitch a number of additional lines next to the first sewn line, stopping and starting at the edge of the paper image.

5. Trim the ends of any loose threads on the front and inside of the card.

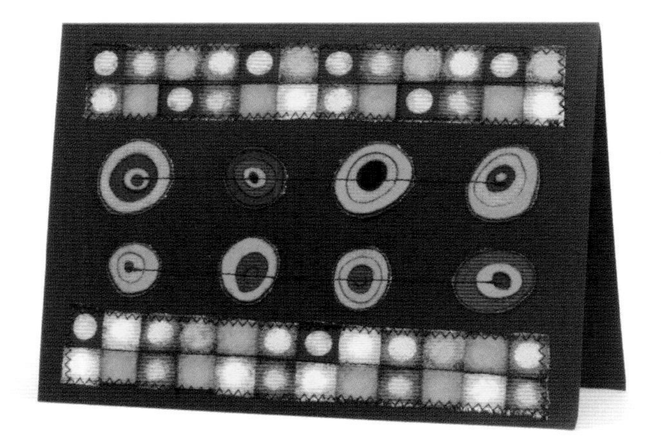

Many Circles

Have fun playing with different sizes and shapes of circles, including circles inside squares.

MATERIALS

- Rectangular landscape black card stock, folded
- 8 fabric circles (smaller than 1 inch [2.5 cm] in diameter)
- 2 strips of fabric with circular pattern, shorter than the width of your card
- Black thread, for sewing and bobbin

INSTRUCTIONS

1. Hold the card open and flat, face up.
2. Place one strip of fabric near the bottom of the card.
3. Stitch straight stitches in the center of the fabric.
4. Stitch zigzag stitches around the edge of the fabric, stitching slowly and stopping briefly to adjust the fabric if it slips out of place.

5. Repeat steps 3 and 4 to attach the second strip near the top of the card.

6. Position two rows of four circles between the two sewn strips. Starting at the center of one of the circles at the end of a row, stitch a line through the next three circles, ending in the center of the fourth circle.

7. Stitch the second row of circles, following step 6.

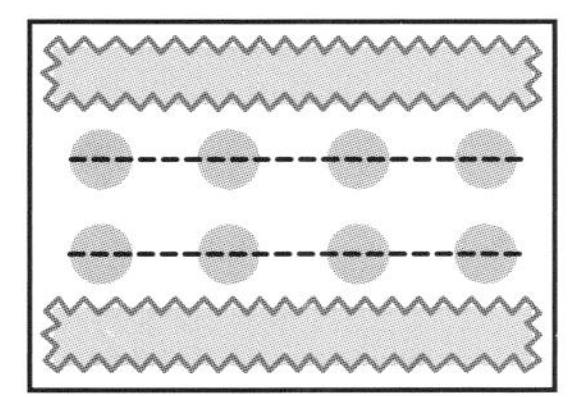

8. Trim the ends of any loose threads on the front and inside of the card.

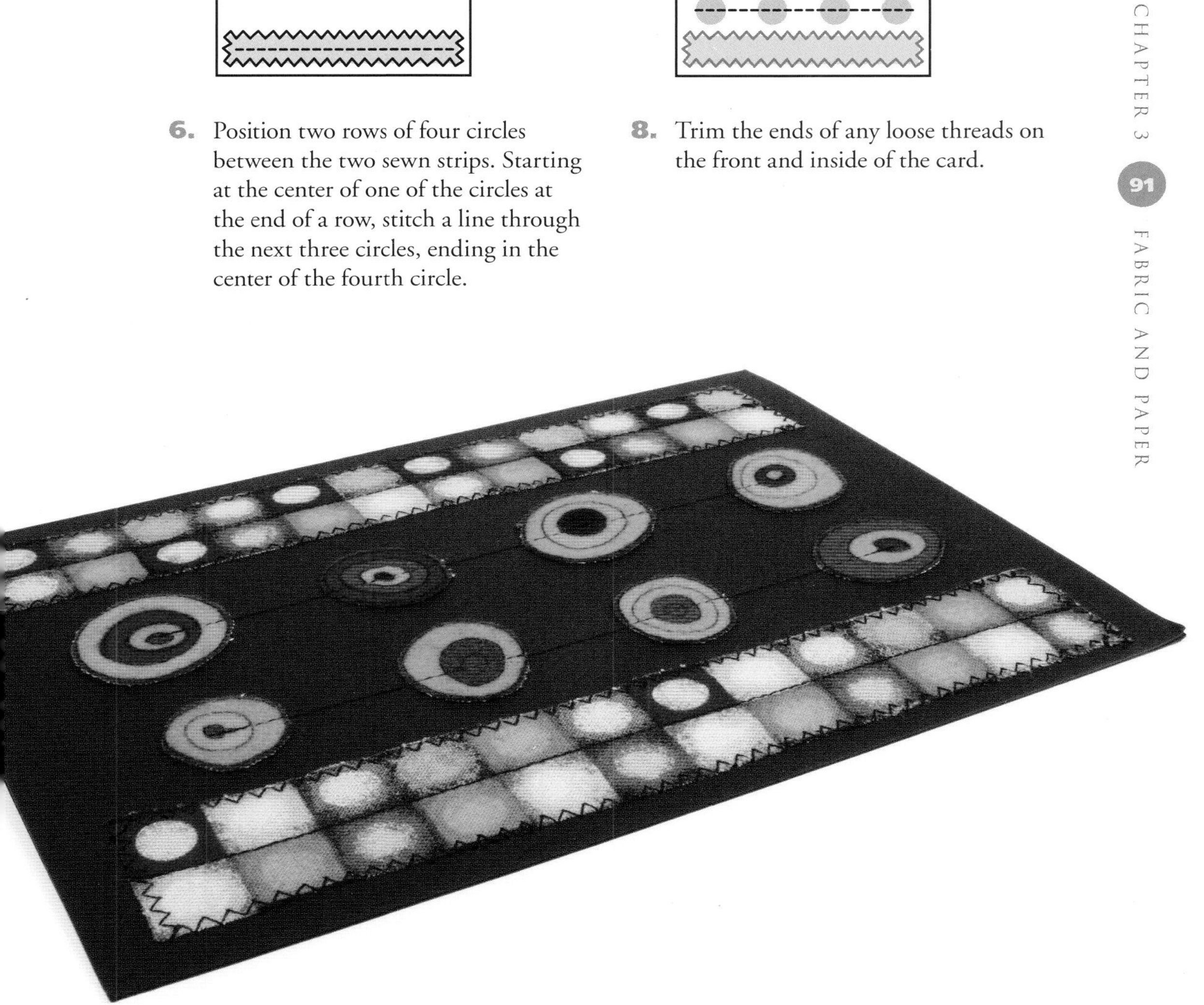

Two by Two

A two-by-two square is a simple, quiltlike design.

MATERIALS

- Square green card stock, folded
- 4 (2-inch [5 cm]) square pieces of a patterned fabric (pink works well)
- Pink thread, for sewing
- Green thread, for bobbin

INSTRUCTIONS

1. Hold the card open and flat, face up.
2. Position the four squares two by two on the card front, leaving some space between them.
3. Sew zigzag stitches on the inside edges on the left and right columns of squares.

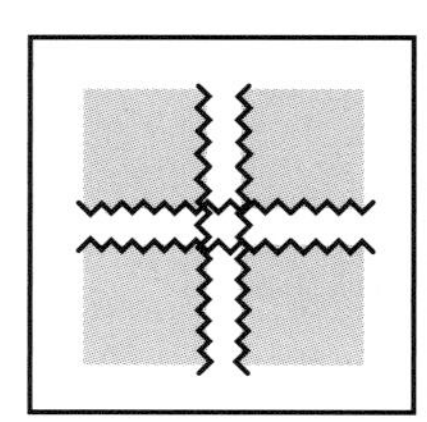

4. Sew zigzag stitches on the inside edges on the top and bottom rows of squares.

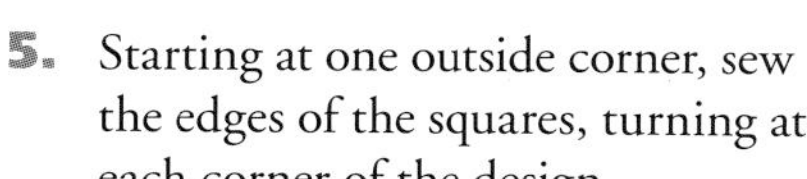

5. Starting at one outside corner, sew the edges of the squares, turning at each corner of the design.

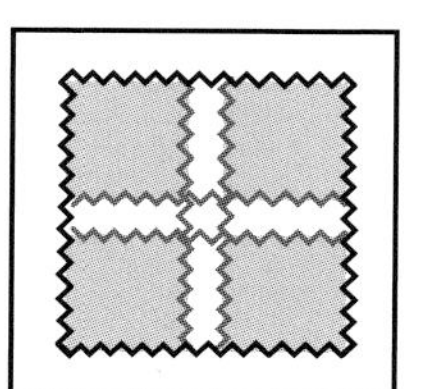

6. Trim the edges of any loose threads on the front and inside of the card.

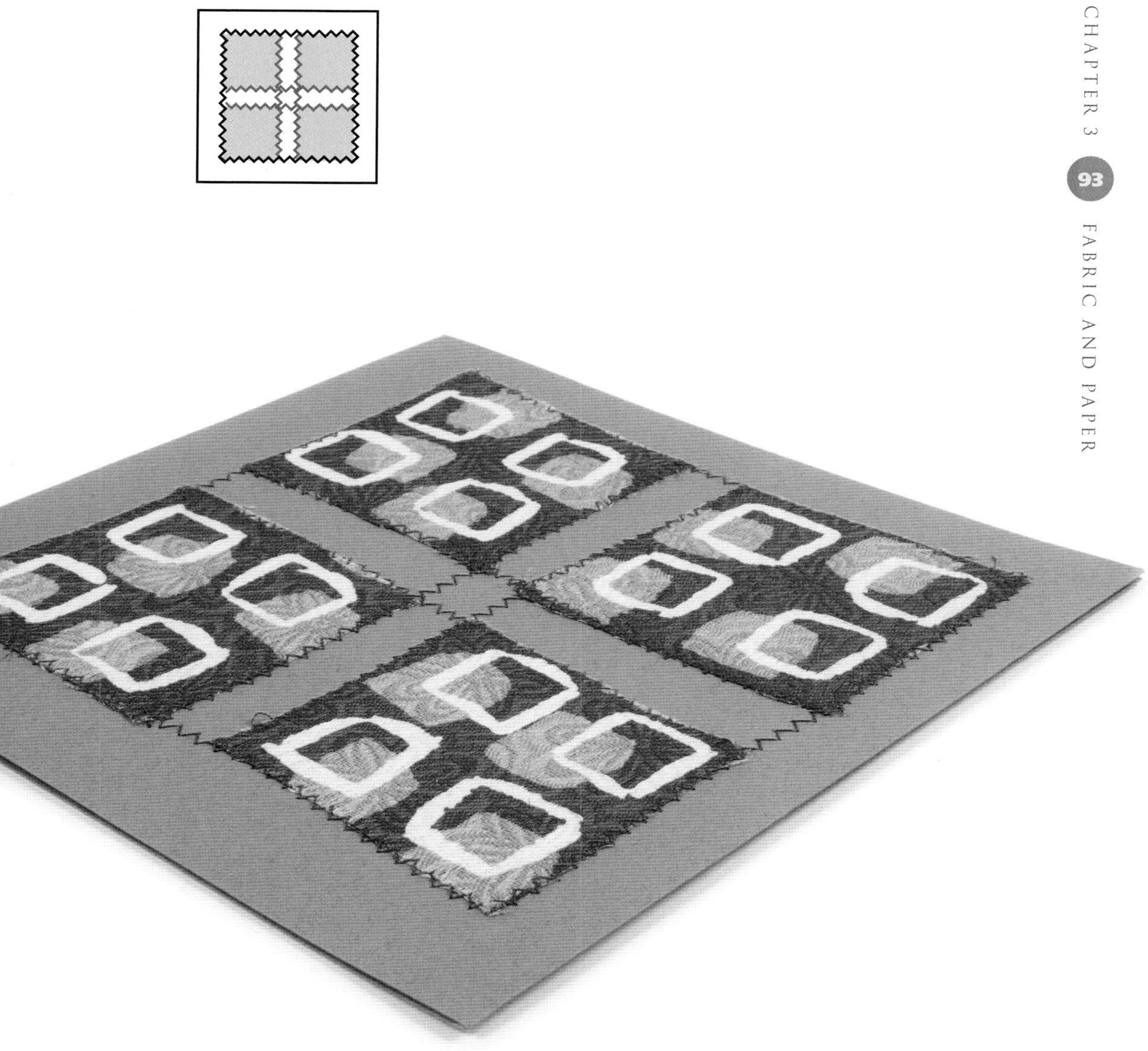

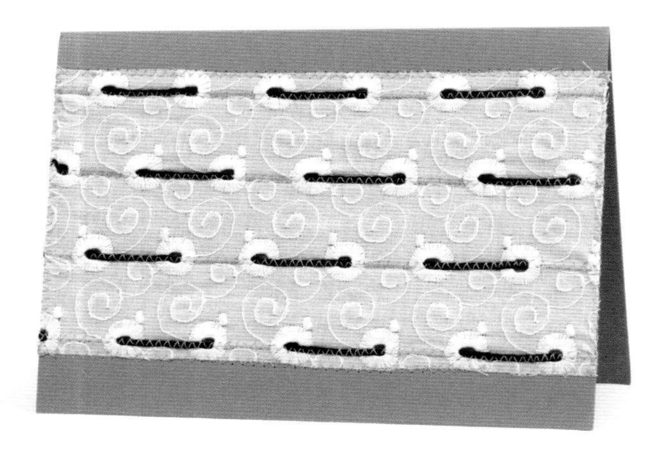

Dashed Lines

Black yarn woven through the holes in eyelet fabric looks like dashed lines across the card.

MATERIALS

- Rectangular landscape gray card stock, folded
- Strip of white eyelet fabric, longer than the width of the card and at least 3 inches (7.5 cm) high
- 12-inch (30.5 cm) lengths of yarn or string (black works well)
- Gray thread, for sewing and bobbin

INSTRUCTIONS

1. Hold the card open and flat, face up.
2. Weave the lengths of yarn or string through the holes in the eyelet fabric.
3. Position the eyelet centered top to bottom on the card front, with the fabric and yarn hanging over the side edges.

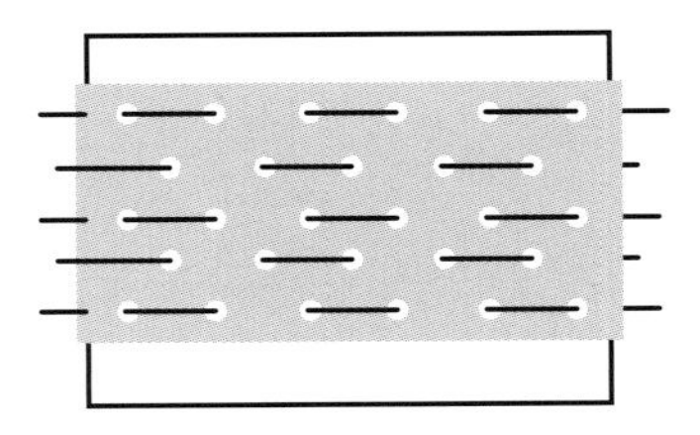

4. Starting at one edge of the card, sew zigzag stitches over one line of yarn and fabric, to attach it to the card.

5. Repeat, sewing the next three lines of yarn and fabric.

6. Trim the extra fabric and yarn close to both edges of the card stock.

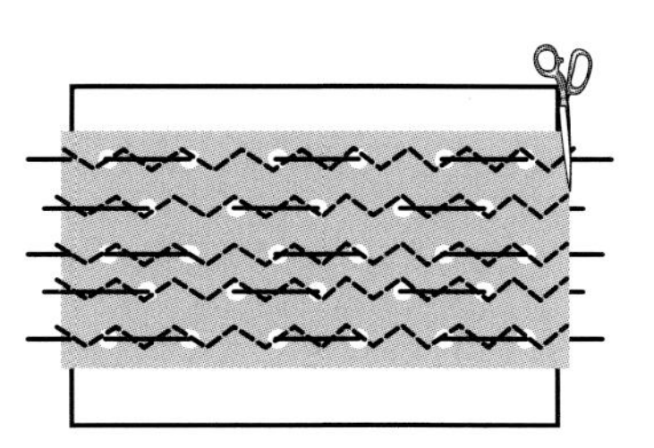

7. Sew zigzag stitches over the raw edges of fabric at the top and bottom, and over both sides, to keep the material in place.

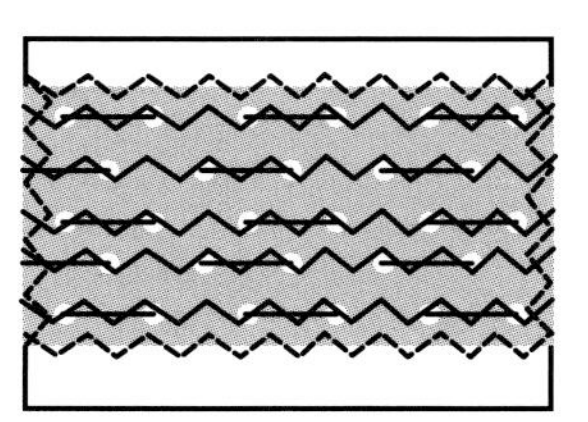

8. Trim the edges of any loose threads on the front and inside of the card.

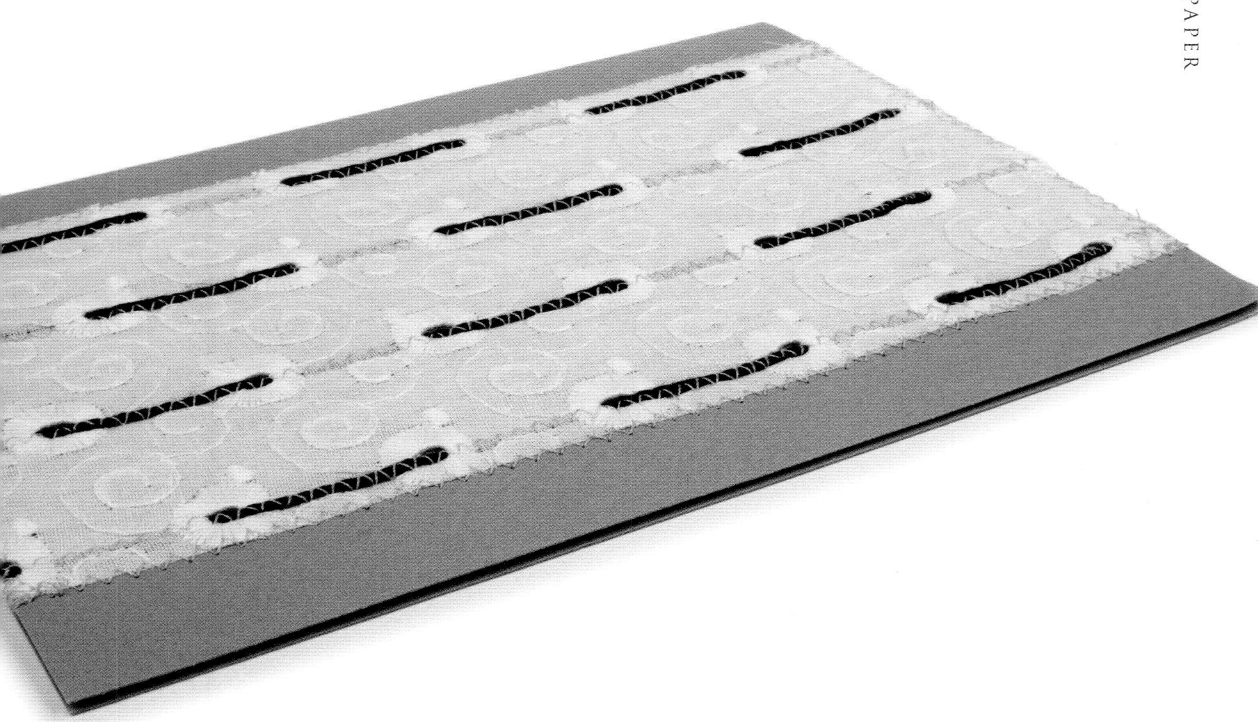

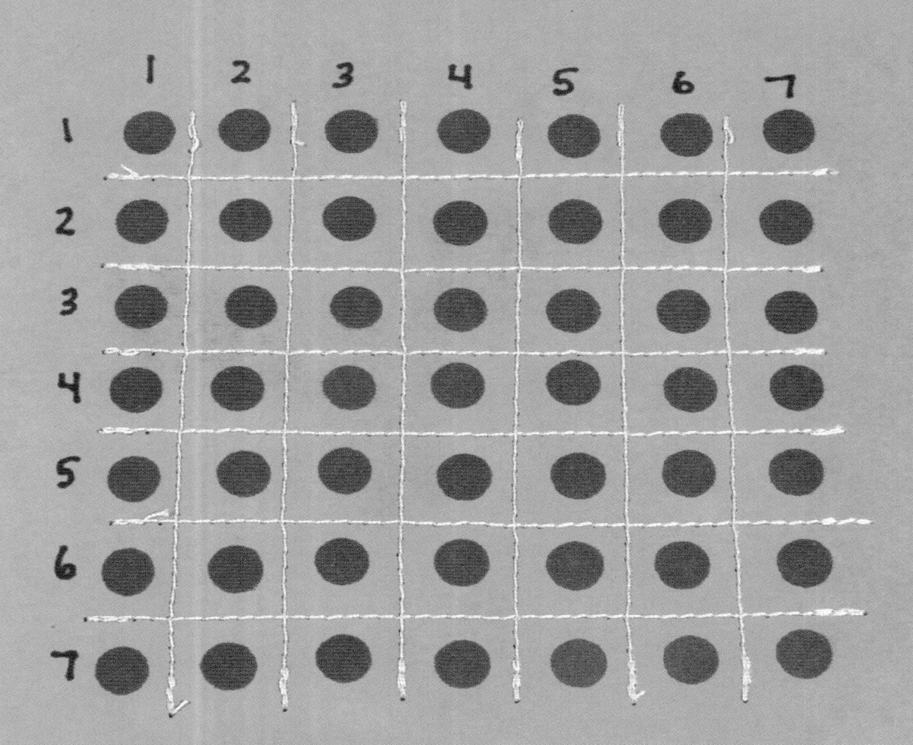
1
2
3
4
5
6
7
1
2
3
4
5
6
7

CHAPTER 4

Surface Design

Surface design is my most favorite art form, whether for decorating cards or wrapping paper, or for incorporation into my own artwork. I have been hand stamping with rubber erasers for as long as I can remember. During my teenage years, I made rubbings of gravestones in a cemetery that dated back to the late 1600s, and because of that, I have a long history of using crayons to create rubbings of different surface textures and objects.

There are many ways to hand stamp designs. When I think of stamping, my first thoughts are about using rubber erasers, both carved and uncarved. Erasers are inexpensive and easy to find, which makes them especially desirable to me. I have included instructions on how to carve erasers (see page 14), and I hope you will give it a try and that you enjoy it.

If you don't feel comfortable carving erasers, you can buy shaped erasers. These erasers, commonly designed for children, come in all kinds of shapes, including hearts and flowers.

If you want to stamp extremely small shapes, consider using the eraser end of a pencil. You can use it as is (a circle), or cut into it with an X-Acto knife, to change its shape to something else.

To stamp irregular textures, try using bunched-up waxed paper and aluminum foil. I recently tried doing this, and I enjoyed it because the textures were very different than anything I could have carved or purchased.

Speaking of purchased, there is no shortage of available ready-made stamp patterns and images. Craft stores have stamping areas, and there are also many websites where you will find just about anything you can imagine.

Crayon rubbings are a fun way to get a texture and pattern on paper, without any mess or fuss, and it's really simple to do. Simply put a piece of paper over what you'd like to get the rubbing of, and slowly move your crayon back and forth over it, pressing harder if it's not showing up as you wish.

When you think of stencils, you might think of using them with brushes and paint, but I enjoy tracing stencils. It's very neat and simple to do and can be enjoyed by children of many ages, as well as adults.

Another surface design technique is to sew a shape or pattern on the card stock and then color it in. You can color it with any dry media you have on hand, such as crayons, markers, Cray-Pas, and more.

Although it might be intimidating to start decorating a blank piece of paper, I hope you will see it as a fun challenge. The supplies are inexpensive and most can easily be found in your home or office. Whether you are a beginner or have lots of design experience, I hope you will enjoy trying these techniques. I hope you are inspired not only to try them, but that you will also search out and try using additional surface design materials and techniques.

Hearts Squared

Share your love by stamping hearts in a grid pattern.

MATERIALS

- Square off-white card stock, folded
- 1 (1 x 1 x 1-inch [2.5 x 2.5 x 2.5 cm]) rubber eraser, cut into a heart shape (see page 14)
- Red inked stamp pad
- Red thread, for sewing
- Cream thread, for bobbin

INSTRUCTIONS

1. Hold the card open and flat, face up.
2. Ink the heart-shaped eraser and press it on the card stock, centering it top and bottom. Refer to page 14 for technique suggestions.

3. Repeat so there are three rows and columns of hearts printed as a grid on the paper.

4. Allow the ink to dry before proceeding.

5. Using the presser foot as a guide, sew a square around the heart images.

6. Trim the ends of any loose threads on the front and inside of the card.

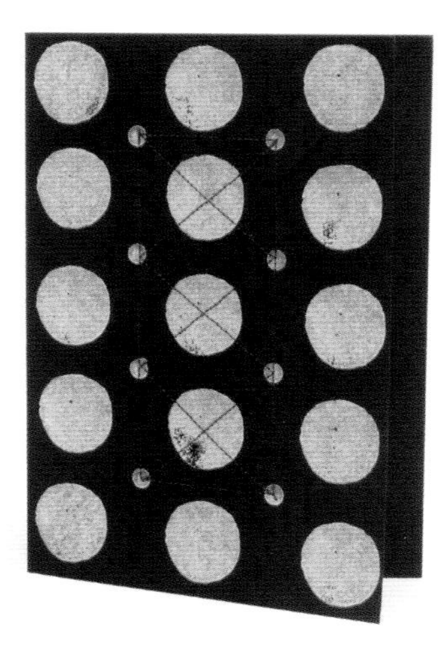

Stamped Circles Pattern

Create a grid pattern with two sizes of circles, and add more geometry with contrasting stitching.

MATERIALS

- Rectangular portrait black card stock, folded
- 1 (1 x 1 x 1-inch [2.5 x 2.5 x 2.5 cm]) rubber eraser, cut into a circular shape (see page 14)
- 1 pencil with unused eraser
- White inked stamp pad
- Red thread, for sewing
- Black thread, for bobbin

INSTRUCTIONS

1. Hold the card open and flat, face up.
2. Press the circular eraser into the inked stamp pad. Press the inked stamp near one corner of the card stock. Refer to page 15 for technique suggestions.
3. Re-ink and repeat so five rows of three circles per row are stamped on the card stock.

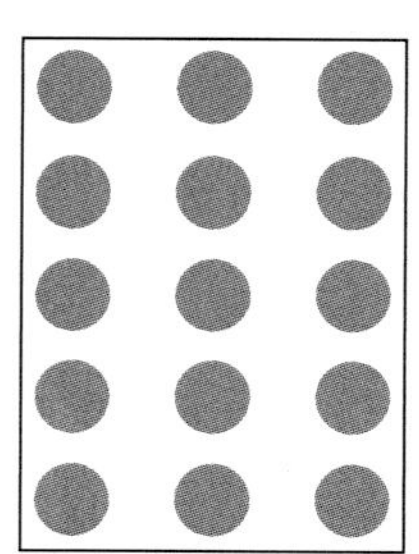

4. Using the eraser end of a pencil, press it into the inked stamp pad and stamp the eraser between the larger circle design, re-inking before printing each dot. Allow the ink to dry before proceeding.

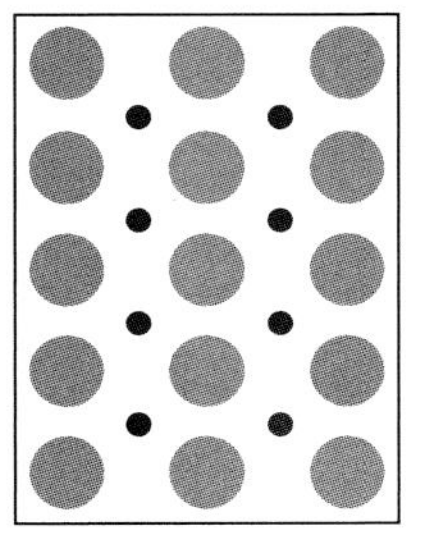

5. Starting at one of the corner-stamped eraser dots, sew a straight line through each dot, turning at the corners, to create a rectangle.

6. Crisscross a straight line from one dot to another dot across the big circles in the middle of the card, creating three big X's.

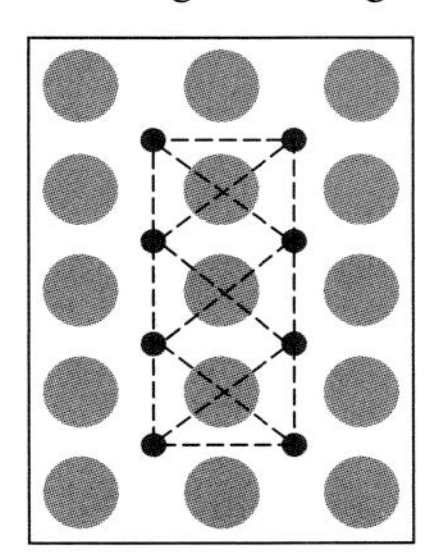

7. Trim the ends of any loose threads on the front and inside of the card.

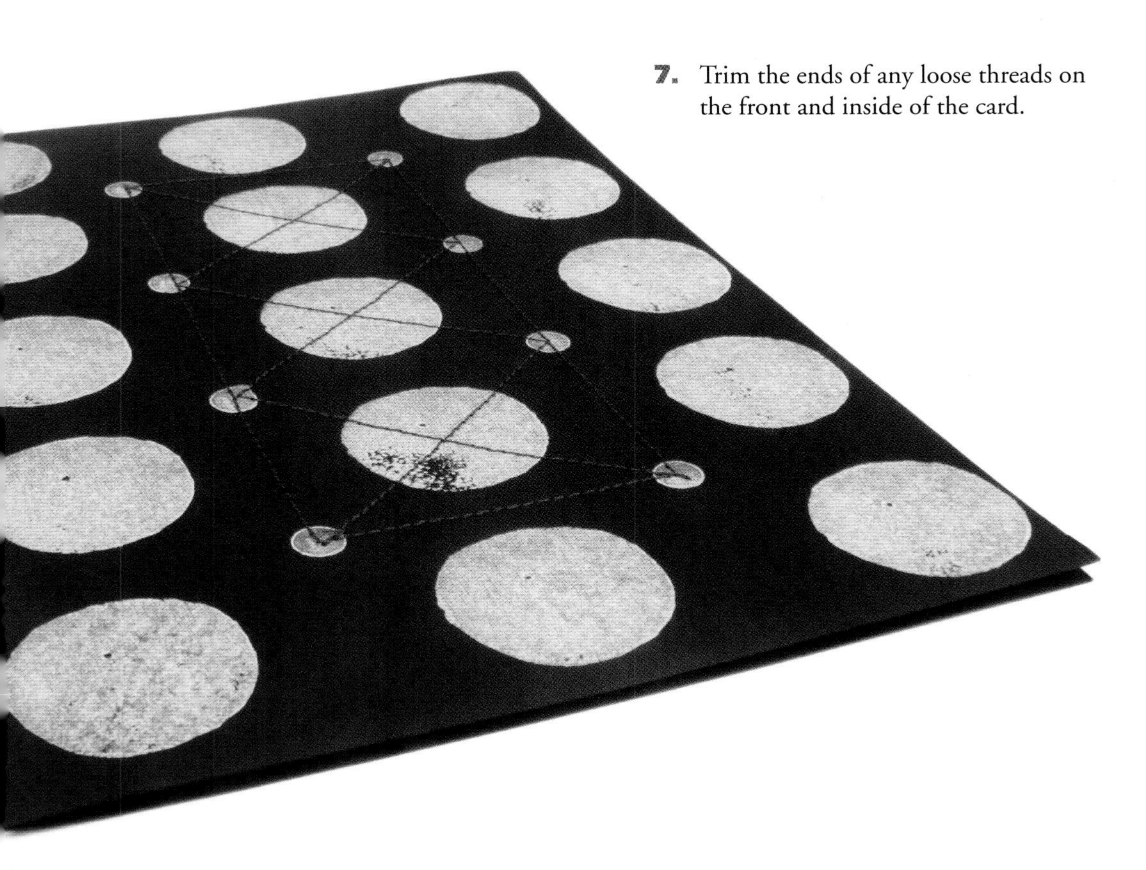

Three Flowers

Try stamping with children's erasers. They come in many shapes and offer many fun design possibilities.

MATERIALS

- Rectangular landscape curry yellow card stock, folded
- 1 flower-shaped purchased rubber eraser
- 1 pencil with an unused eraser
- Red inked stamp pad
- White inked stamp pad
- Green thread, for sewing
- Yellow thread, for bobbin
- Optional: Green marker or colored pencil

INSTRUCTIONS

1. Hold the card open and flat, face up.
2. Press the flower-shaped eraser into the red inked stamp pad. Press the inked stamp on the card stock, centering it near the top of the card. Refer to page 15 for technique suggestions.
3. Repeat so a row of three flower shapes is printed on the paper. Allow the ink to dry before proceeding.

4. Using the eraser end of a pencil, press it into the white inked stamp pad and stamp the eraser in the middle of each flower design, re-inking before printing each dot. Allow the ink to dry before proceeding.

5. Using a straight stitch, sew a stem and two leaves at the bottom of each flower. Color in the leaves and stem, using a green marker or colored pencil, if you wish.

6. Trim the ends of any loose threads on the front and inside of the card.

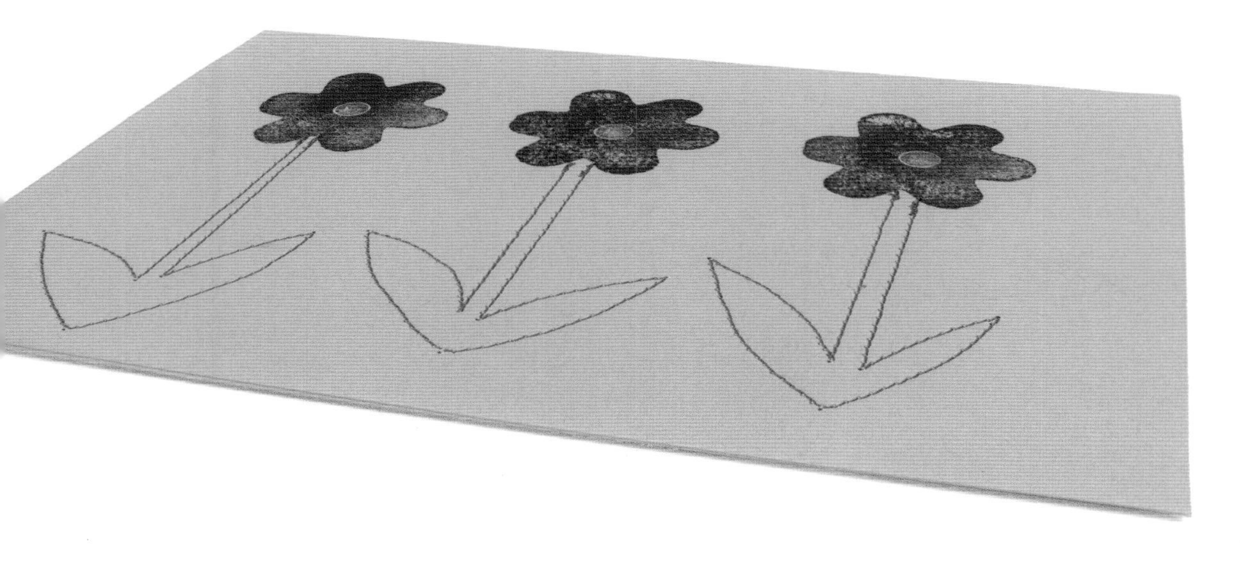

Rotated Block Print

Rotating the shape while rubber-stamping provides many options for creating different designs.

MATERIALS

- Rectangular portrait purple card stock, folded
- 1 (1 x 1 x 1-inch [2.5 x 2.5 x 2.5 cm]) rubber eraser, with a thin line removed down the middle so it has a double bar shape (see page 14)
- Green inked stamp pad
- Green thread, for sewing
- Purple thread, for bobbin

INSTRUCTIONS

1. Hold the card open and flat, face up.
2. Press the stamp into the inked stamp pad. Press the inked stamp near one corner of the card stock. Refer to page 15 for technique suggestions.

3. Re-ink and repeat, rotating the stamp 90 degrees each time. When you are finished, five rows with four stamps per row should be stamped on the card. Allow the ink to dry before proceeding.

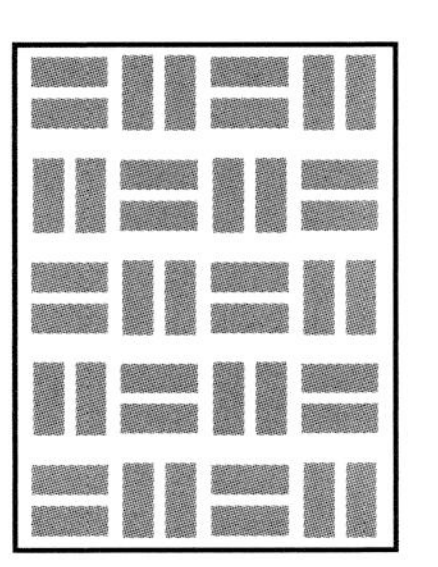

4. Sew a straight line between each row of stamps, from one end of the card to the other.

5. Rotate the card and repeat sewing between each row.

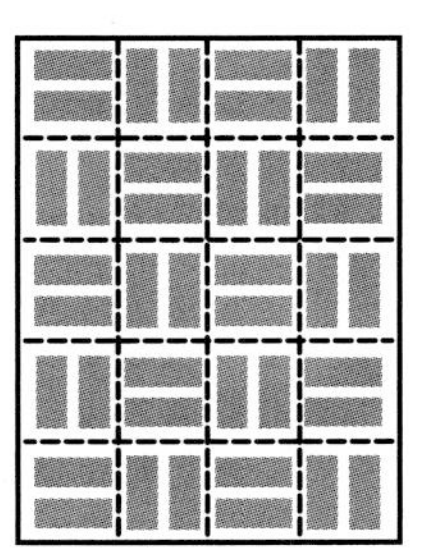

6. Trim the ends of any loose threads on the front and inside of the card.

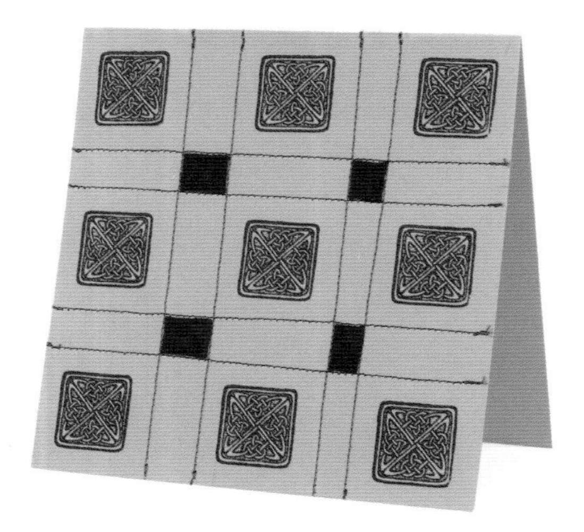

Quilt Pattern

Amish quilts were an inspiration for this quiltlike pattern.

MATERIALS

- Square light blue card stock
- 1 purchased patterned stamp
- Blue inked stamp pad
- 1 ultrafine blue marker
- Orange thread, for sewing
- Light blue thread, for bobbin

INSTRUCTIONS

1. Hold the card open and flat, face up.
2. Press the stamp into the inked stamp pad. Press the inked stamp near one corner of the card stock. Refer to page 15 for technique suggestions.
3. Re-ink and repeat stamping in each corner of the card. Repeat by stamping the top, bottom, and left and right sides in the middle, and in the very center of the card. Allow the ink to dry before proceeding.

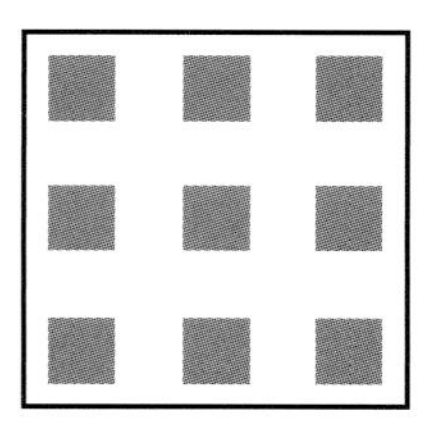

4. Using the presser foot of the sewing machine as a guide, sew straight lines at the right and left edges of the stamped patterns, from one end of the card to the other, between each row of stamps.

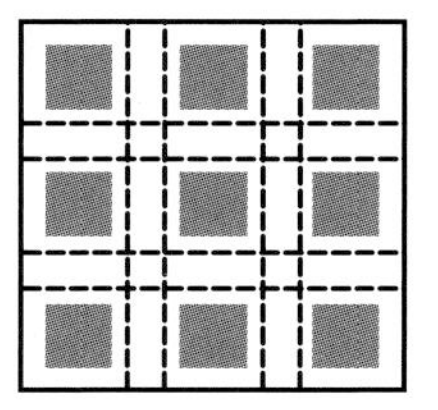

5. Rotate the card and repeat sewing at the right and left edges between each row.

6. Fill in all four stitched squares, using an ultrafine blue marker.

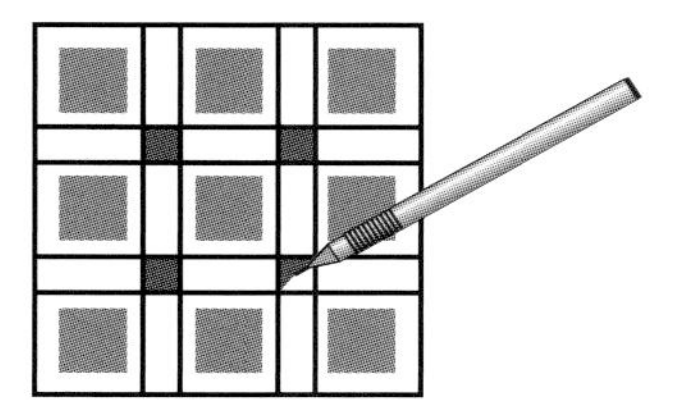

7. Trim the ends of any loose threads on the front and inside of the card.

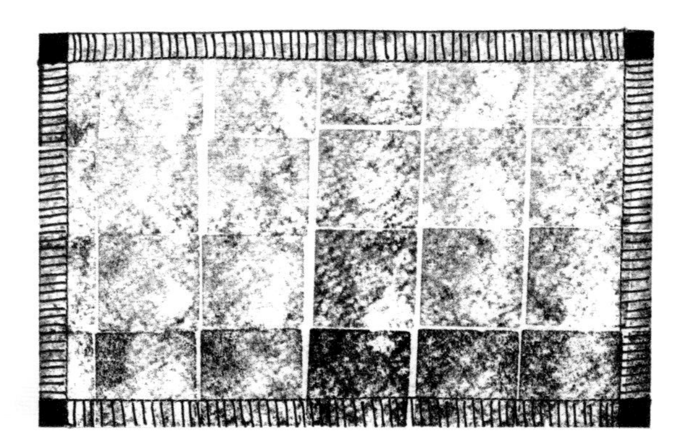

Stamped Postcard

Plain white postcards are a blank slate waiting to be decorated.

MATERIALS

- Rectangular white postcard
- 1 (1 x 1 x 1-inch [2.5 x 2.5 x 2.5 cm]) square rubber eraser
- Black inked stamp pad
- 1 ultrafine black marker
- Black thread, for sewing
- White thread, for bobbin

INSTRUCTIONS

1. Hold the card open and flat, face up.
2. Press the stamp into the inked stamp pad. Press the inked stamp near the bottom center of the card stock. Without re-inking, stamp again immediately above, again above that, and once again above that, creating four stamped impressions that are progressively lighter. Refer to page 15 for technique suggestions.

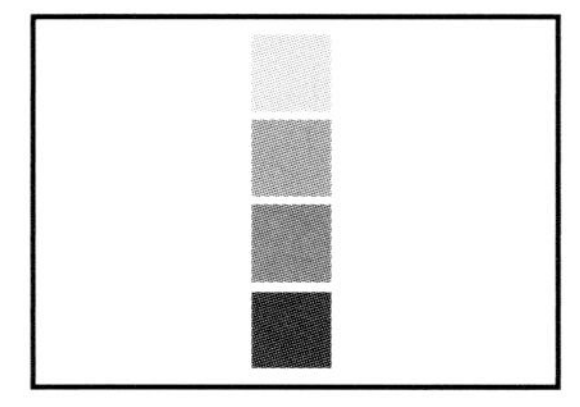

3. Re-ink and repeat stamping again to the left and right of the first column, re-inking only for the bottom impression for each column. Allow the ink to dry before proceeding.

4. Using the presser foot of the sewing machine as a guide, sew straight lines at the right, left, top, and bottom edges of the card.

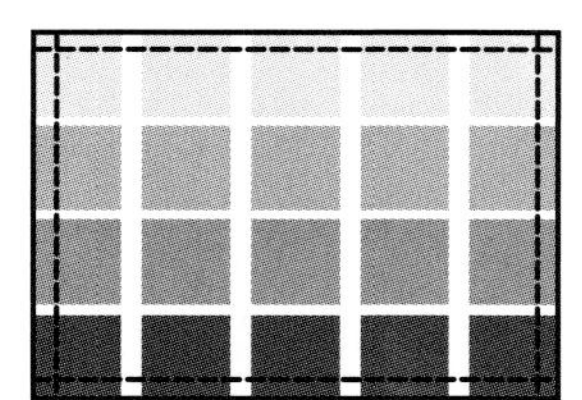

5. Fill in all four stitched squares in the corner, using an ultrafine black marker.

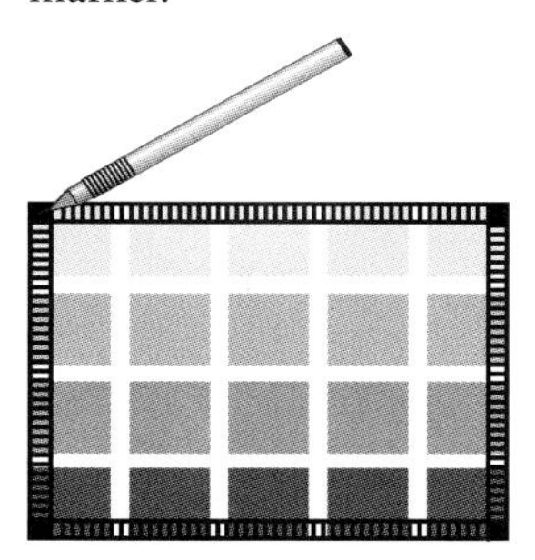

6. Use the marker to draw many short lines from the stitching to the outer edges of the card.

7. Trim the ends of any loose threads on the front and inside of the card.

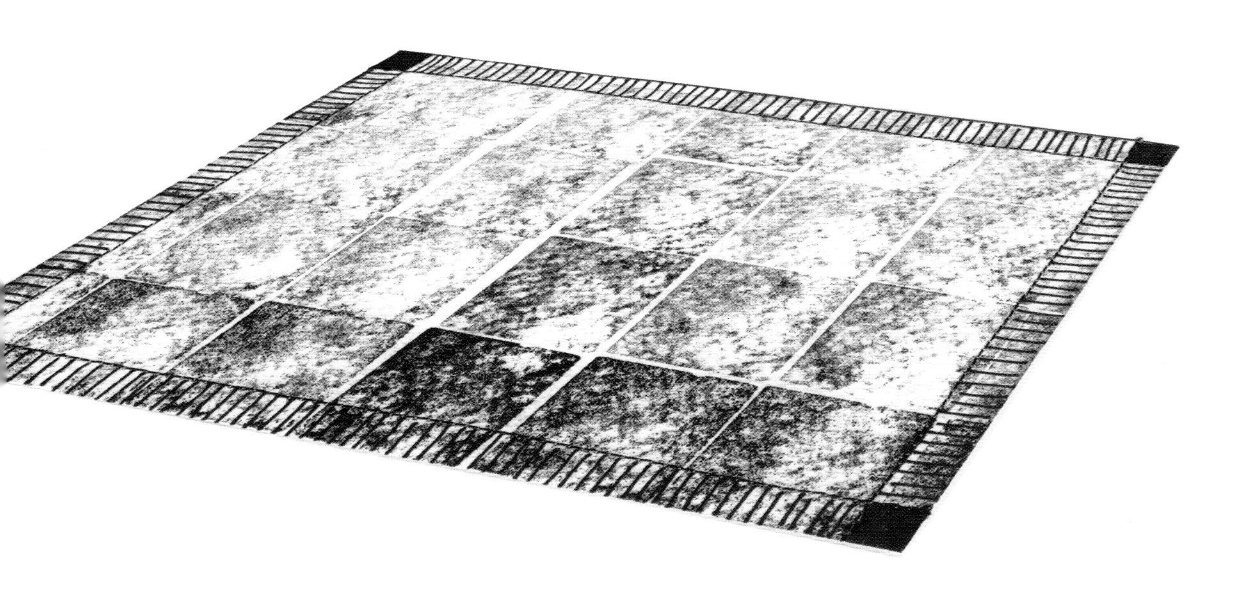

Repeat Printed Postcard

Add color to a white postcard by printing with waxed paper and aluminum foil and by appliquéing different-colored paper.

MATERIALS

- Rectangular white postcard
- 1 waxed paper stamp (see page 16)
- 1 aluminum foil stamp (see page 16)
- 1 (6 x 3-inch [15 x 7.5 cm]) piece of yellow card stock
- Green inked stamp pad
- Blue inked stamp pad
- White thread, for sewing and bobbin

INSTRUCTIONS

1. Hold the card open and flat, face up.
2. Press the waxed paper stamp into the green inked stamp pad. Print the inked waxed paper in a pattern or randomly on the postcard. Re-ink, and stamp again and again on the paper until the desired effect is achieved. Refer to page 15 for technique suggestions.

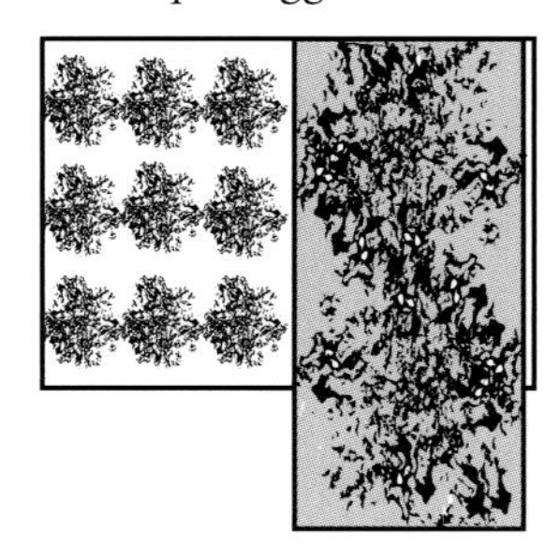

3. Press the foil stamp into the blue inked stamp pad.

4. Print the inked foil in a pattern or randomly on the yellow card stock. Re-ink, and stamp again and again on the paper until the desired effect is achieved. Allow the ink to dry before proceeding.

5. Place the dry printed yellow paper vertically on the white postcard.

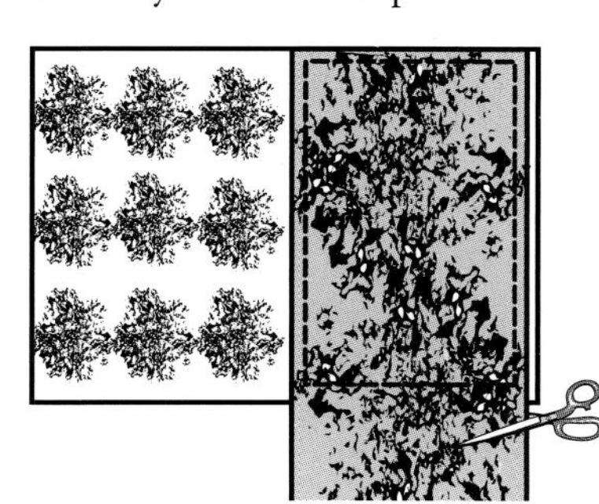

6. Using the presser foot of the sewing machine as a guide, sew straight lines around the top, right, and bottom edges and center of the white printed postcard, so the top section of the yellow paper is attached.

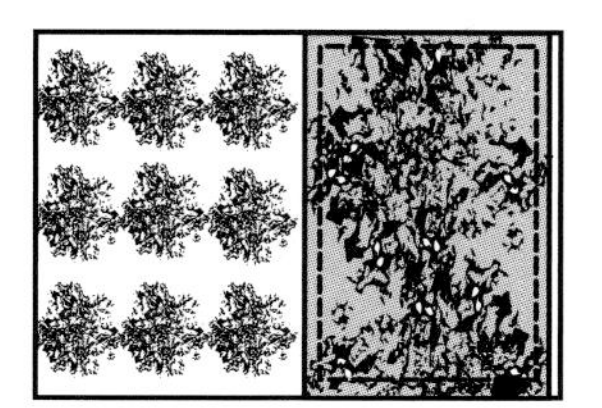

7. Trim the yellow paper at the bottom edge of the postcard.

8. Trim the ends of any loose threads on the front and inside of the card.

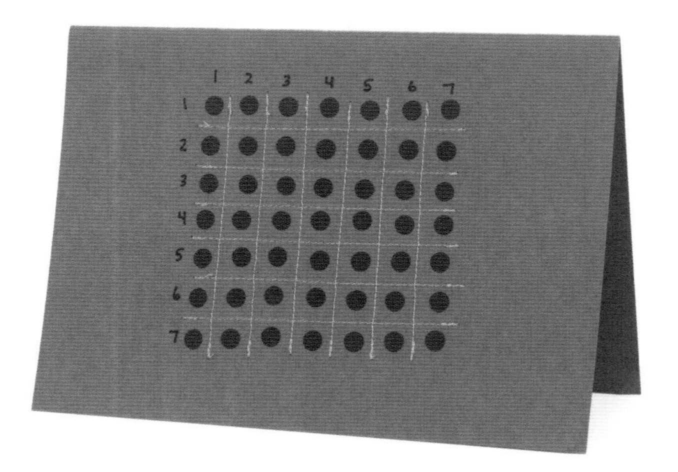

Birthday Dots

Use stamped dots to mark the years on a birthday card. Divide the age of the celebrant into a convenient number of rows, to make your design.

MATERIALS

- Rectangular landscape turquoise card stock, folded
- 1 pencil with unused eraser
- Red inked stamp pad
- 1 ultrafine black marker
- Ruler
- Yellow thread, for sewing
- Turquoise thread, for bobbin

INSTRUCTIONS

1. Hold the card open and flat, face up.
2. Using the eraser end of a pencil, press it into the red inked stamp pad and stamp the eraser every half inch along the horizontal (use the ruler as a guide), re-inking before printing each dot.

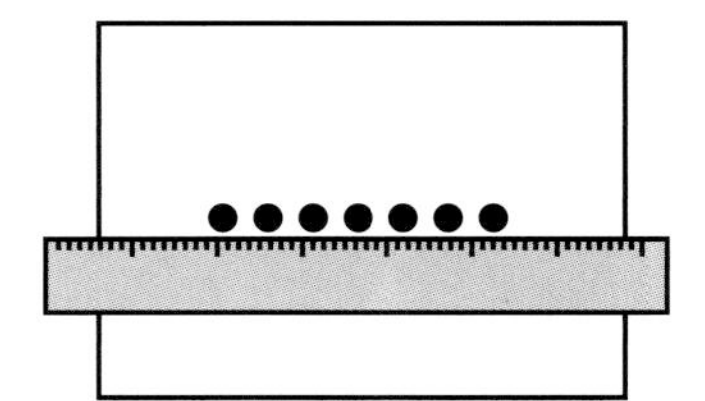

3. Hold the ruler vertically to the left of the first row of dots on the card, and using the eraser end of a pencil, stamp the eraser every half inch along the vertical, re-inking before printing each dot.

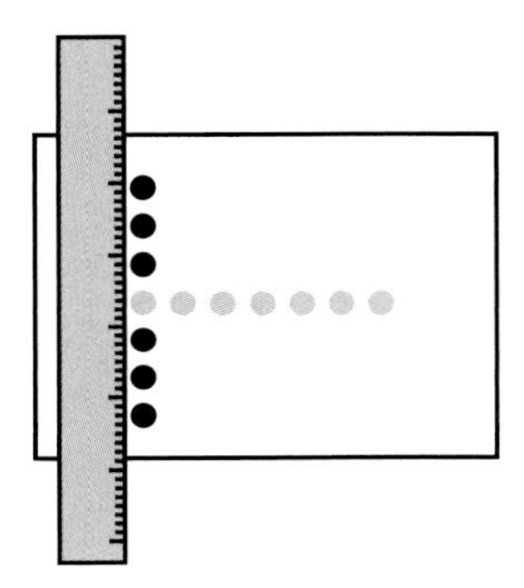

4. Stamp the rest of the dots by eye, using the previous dots as a guide. Re-ink before printing each dot. Allow the ink to dry before proceeding.

5. Starting at one edge and ending at the other, sew a straight line between each row of stamped dots.

6. Repeat by sewing between each column of stamped dots, starting and stopping at the outer edges.

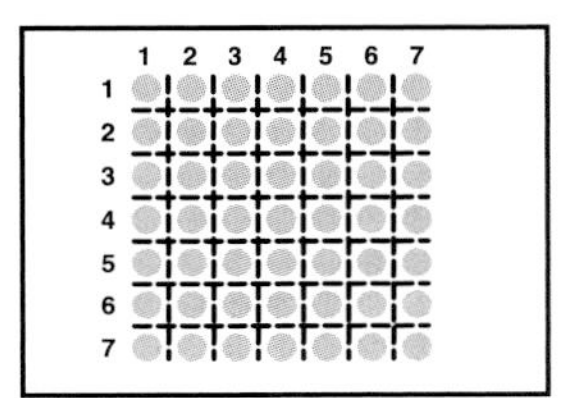

7. Using an ultrafine black marker, number each of the rows and columns at the left and top by hand.

8. Trim the ends of any loose threads on the front and inside of the card.

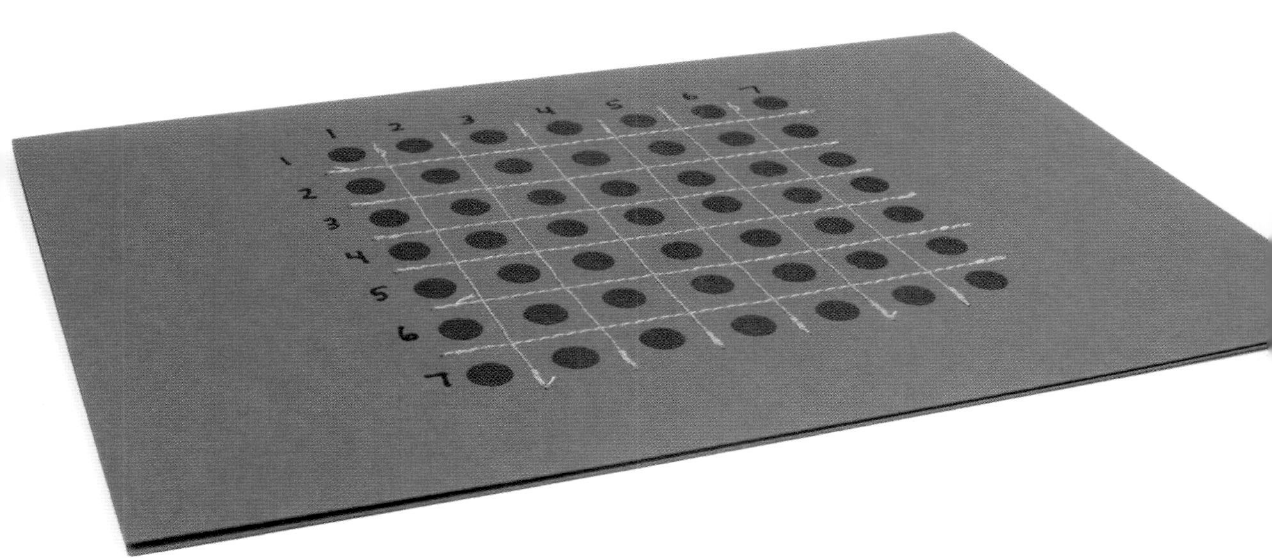

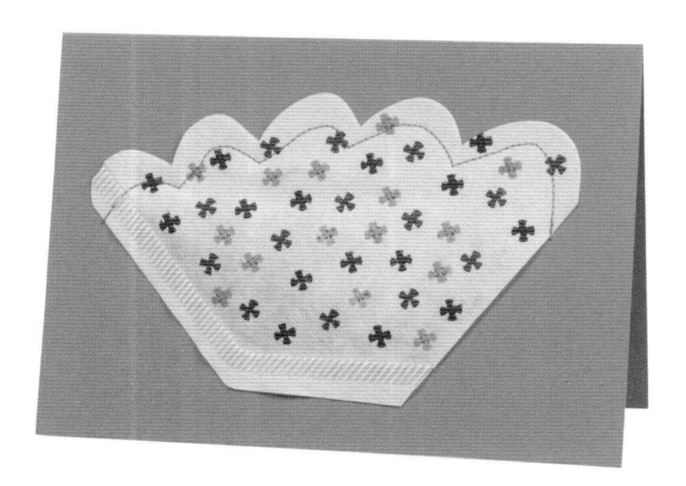

Garden Starter Kit

A card with flower seeds is a garden by mail and can be enjoyed as the flowers bloom all summer long.

MATERIALS

- Rectangular landscape kraft brown card stock, folded
- 1 pencil with an unused eraser cut like a small flower (see page 15)
- Red inked stamp pad
- Magenta inked stamp pad
- Green inked stamp pad
- 1 unused white cone-style coffee filter
- Pair of scissors
- 1 packet of flower seeds
- Khaki brown thread, for sewing and bobbin

INSTRUCTIONS

1. Hold the card open and flat, face up.
2. Place the coffee filter on the work surface.
3. Using the eraser end of the pencil, press it into the red inked stamp pad and stamp randomly on the filter. Re-ink and stamp randomly fifteen times.
4. Clean the stamp each time before changing colors. Repeat using the magenta inked stamp pad and then the green, stamping and re-inking randomly fifteen times for each color. Allow the ink to dry before proceeding.

5. Cut the open end of the coffee filter into rounded petals so it is slightly shorter than it was originally.

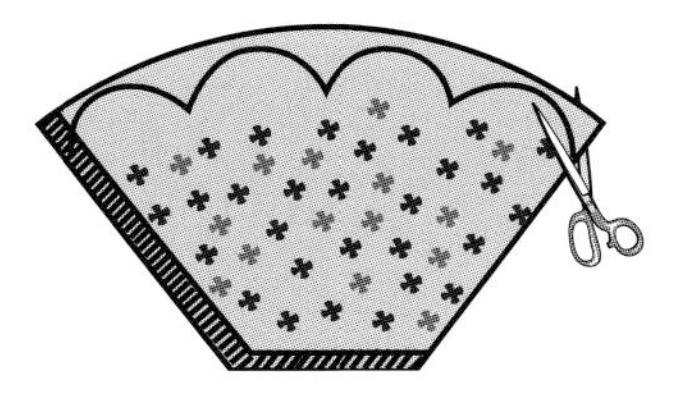

6. Pour the flower seeds from a small packet into the printed coffee filter.

7. Center the flowerlike printed coffee filter on the card. Using the presser foot of the sewing machine as a guide, sew a straight line around the scalloped open edge of the filter, to attach it to the card and secure the seeds inside the filter.

8. Trim the ends of any loose threads on the front and inside of the card.

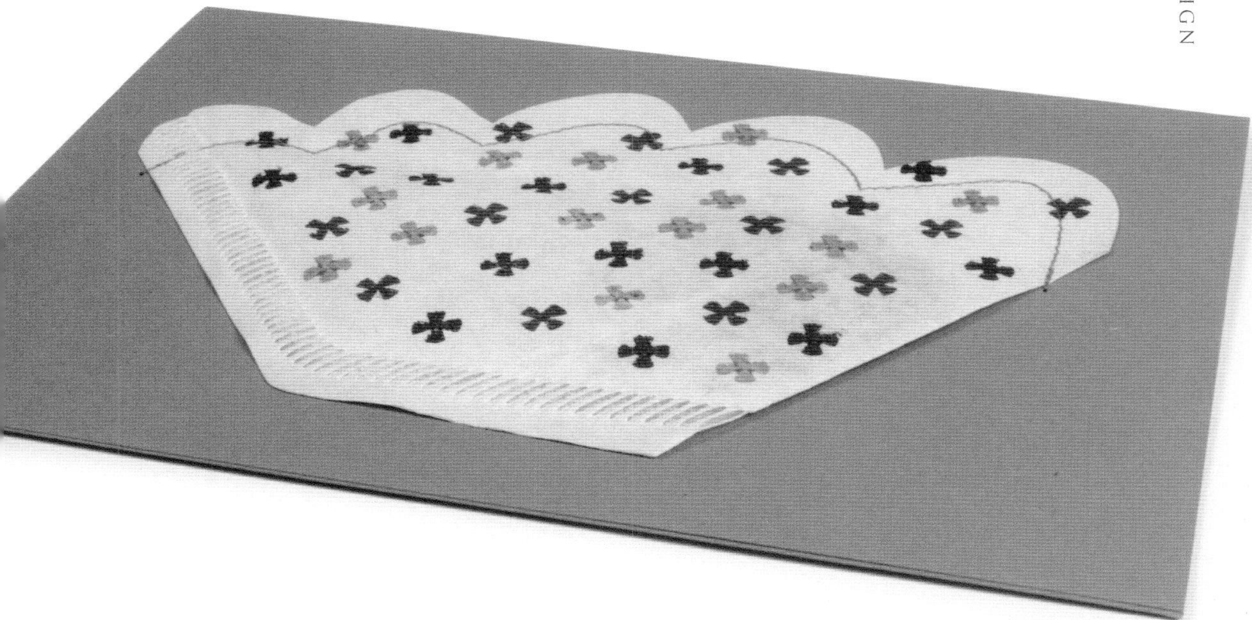

NOTE: *Remember to tell the recipient that there are seeds inside the filter and what kind of seeds they are. The recipient can cut the coffee filter from the card, and either plant the whole coffee filter or sprinkle the seeds from it!*

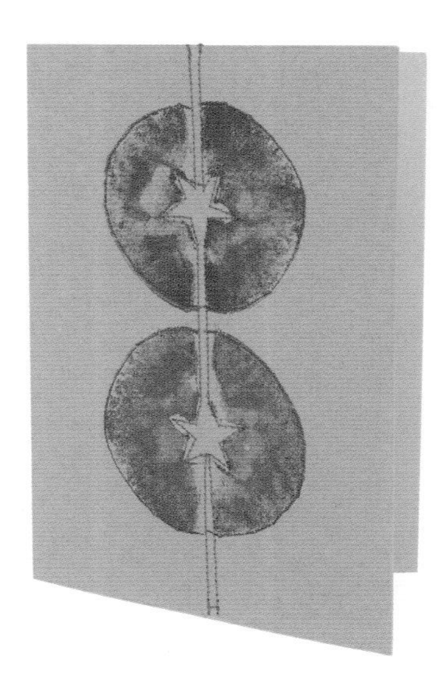

An Apple a Day

The star in the center of an apple makes a fun print for a card, suitable for many different occasions.

MATERIALS

- Rectangular portrait green card stock, folded
- 1/2 small apple, cut through the center star to make two quarters (see page 16)
- Red inked stamp pad
- Green thread, for sewing and bobbin

INSTRUCTIONS

1. Hold the card open and flat, face up.
2. Press the left half, and then the right half, of the star side of the apple stamp into the red inked stamp pad. Refer to page 16 for technique suggestions.

3. Hold the left and right halves together, with the center star halves matching, so they will stamp as one.

4. Press the inked apple firmly in the lower center of the card.

5. Re-ink both the left and right halves of the apple.

6. Holding the left and right halves together again, stamp them firmly on the paper again, centered and slightly above the first apple print. Allow the ink to dry before proceeding.

7. Centering the sewing machine needle above the middle of the right edge of both left apple prints, sew a straight line from the top of the card to the bottom, pivoting and outlining the center star.

8. Sew to the right of the first line of stitching, from the top of the card to the bottom, pivoting and outlining the center star on both right apple prints.

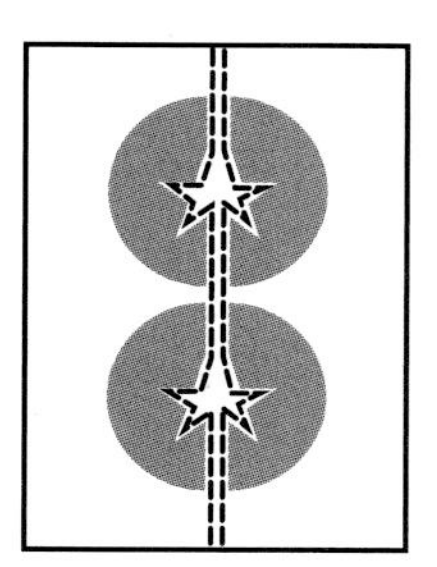

9. Trim the ends of any loose threads on the front and inside of the card.

Flowerlike Citrus Print

Prints made with cut citrus look like flowers.

MATERIALS

- Square curry yellow card stock
- ½ small lemon or lime (see page 16)
- Green inked stamp pad
- Orange thread, for sewing
- Yellow thread, for bobbin

INSTRUCTIONS

1. Hold the card open and flat, face up.
2. Press the lemon stamp into the green inked stamp pad. Print the inked lemon in the upper left corner of the card. Refer to page 16 for technique suggestions.

3. Continue printing to make a three-column by three-row pattern on the card. Re-ink each time before stamping on the paper. Allow the ink to dry before proceeding.

4. Sew straight lines from top to bottom between the two columns of stamped lemons.

5. Sew straight lines from side to side between the rows of lemon prints.

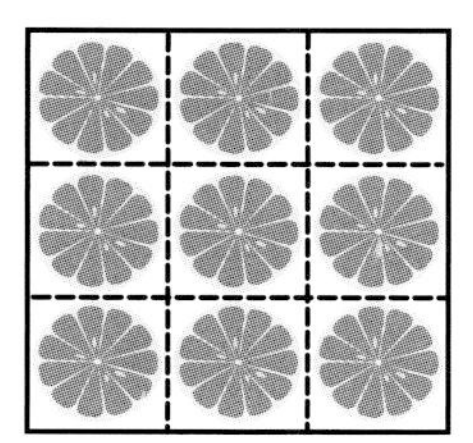

6. Trim the ends of any loose threads on the front and inside of the card.

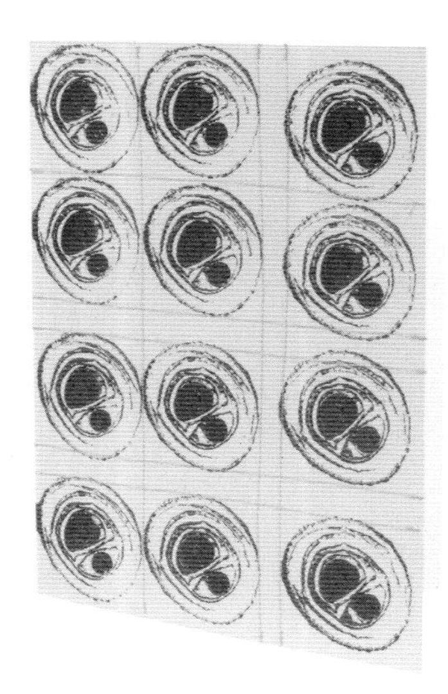

No-Tears Onion Print

Onion prints are very individual and organic. Using onions as a stamp won't make your eyes tear.

MATERIALS

- Rectangular portrait off-white card stock
- 1/2 small onion or shallot (see page 16)
- Red inked stamp pad
- Yellow thread, for sewing
- Off-white thread, for bobbin

INSTRUCTIONS

1. Hold the card open and flat, face up.
2. Press the onion stamp into the red inked stamp pad. Print the inked onion in the upper left corner of the card. Refer to page 16 for technique suggestions.

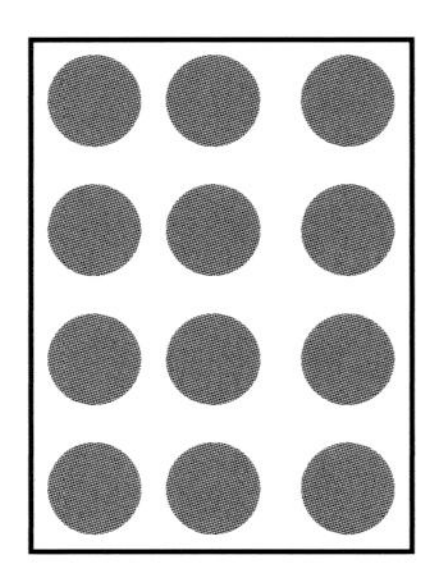

3. Continue printing to make a three-column by four-row pattern on the card. Re-ink each time before stamping on the paper. Leave a little extra space between the second and third columns, between the second and third rows, and between the third and fourth rows. Allow the ink to dry before proceeding.

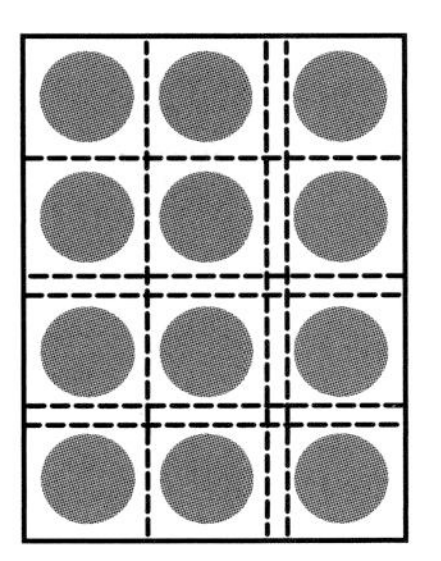

4. Sew straight lines from top to bottom between the left and middle columns. Then sew two rows of lines between the second and third columns.

5. Sew straight lines from side to side between the top two rows of onion prints. Then sew two rows of lines between the second and the third and forth rows of prints.

6. Trim the ends of any loose threads on the front and inside of the card.

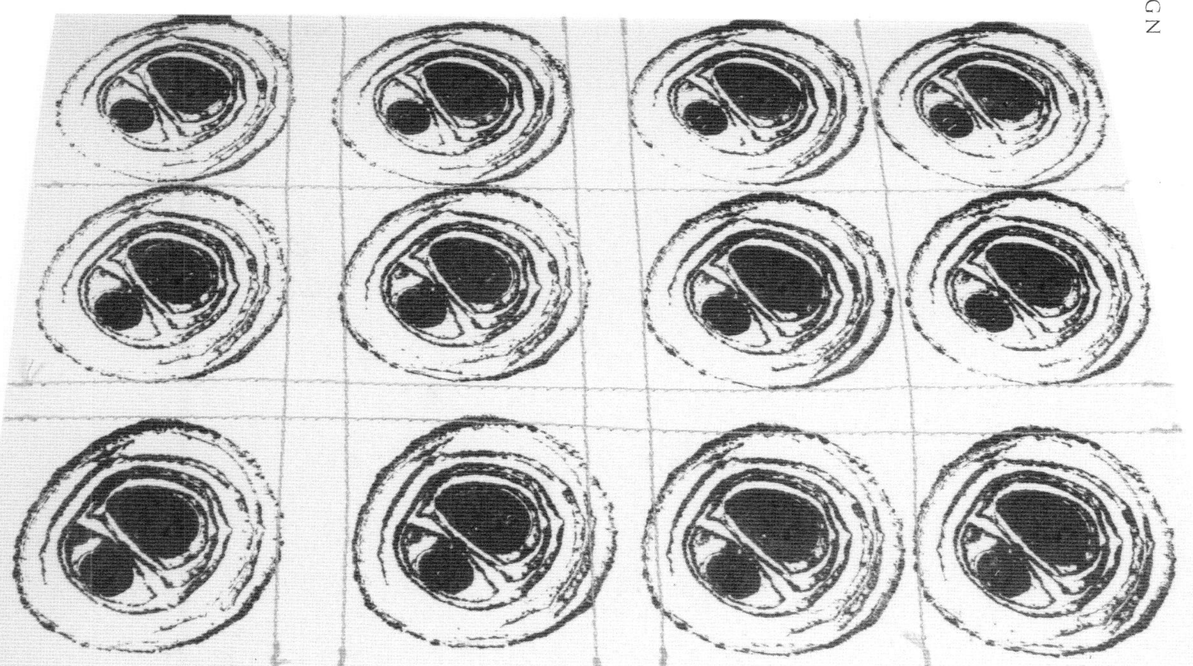

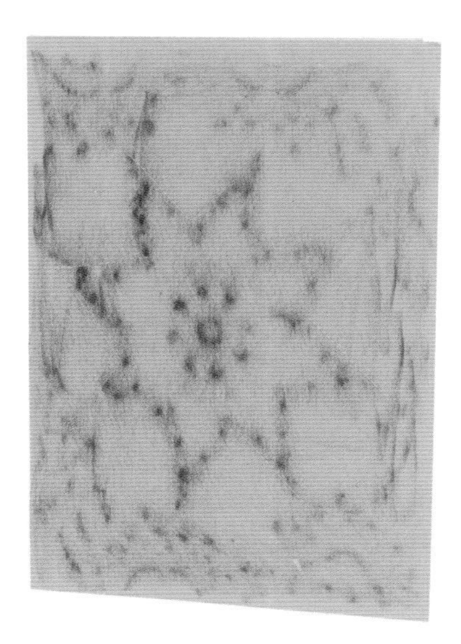

Lace Rubbing

The texture of lace is nice to capture, especially if the actual lace cannot be cut up and used in a project.

MATERIALS

- ◆ Rectangular portrait chartreuse card stock, folded
- ◆ 1 piece of thick lace (or any textured surface)
- ◆ 1 large black crayon
- ◆ Yellow thread, for sewing
- ◆ Chartreuse thread, for bobbin

INSTRUCTIONS

1. Hold the card open and flat, face up.
2. Lay the piece of lace on the work surface.
3. Position the open card over an interesting part of the lace design.

4. Rub the crayon over the card, pressing hard enough to pick up the texture of the lace. Keep rubbing with the crayon until you have the desired amount of texture and crayon color. Refer to page 17 for technique suggestions.

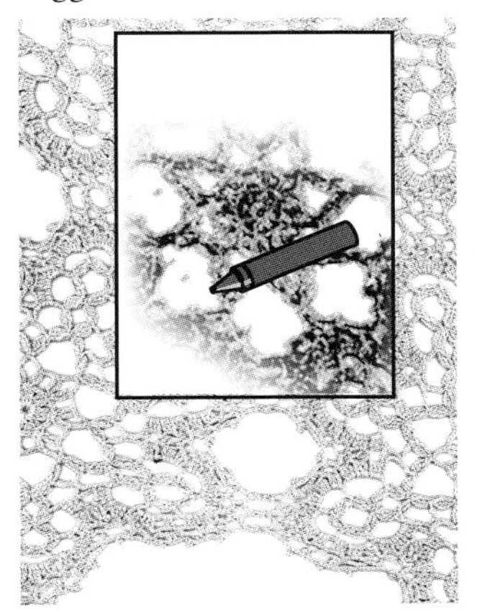

5. Starting at the edge of the main pattern of the rubbing, sew a straight stitch around the pattern, ending the sewing where it began.

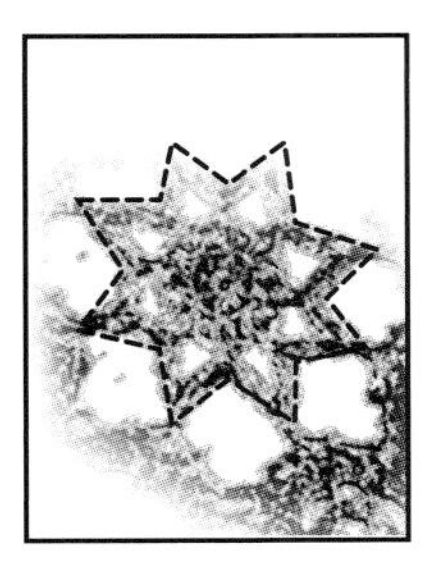

6. Trim the ends of any loose threads on the front and inside of the card.

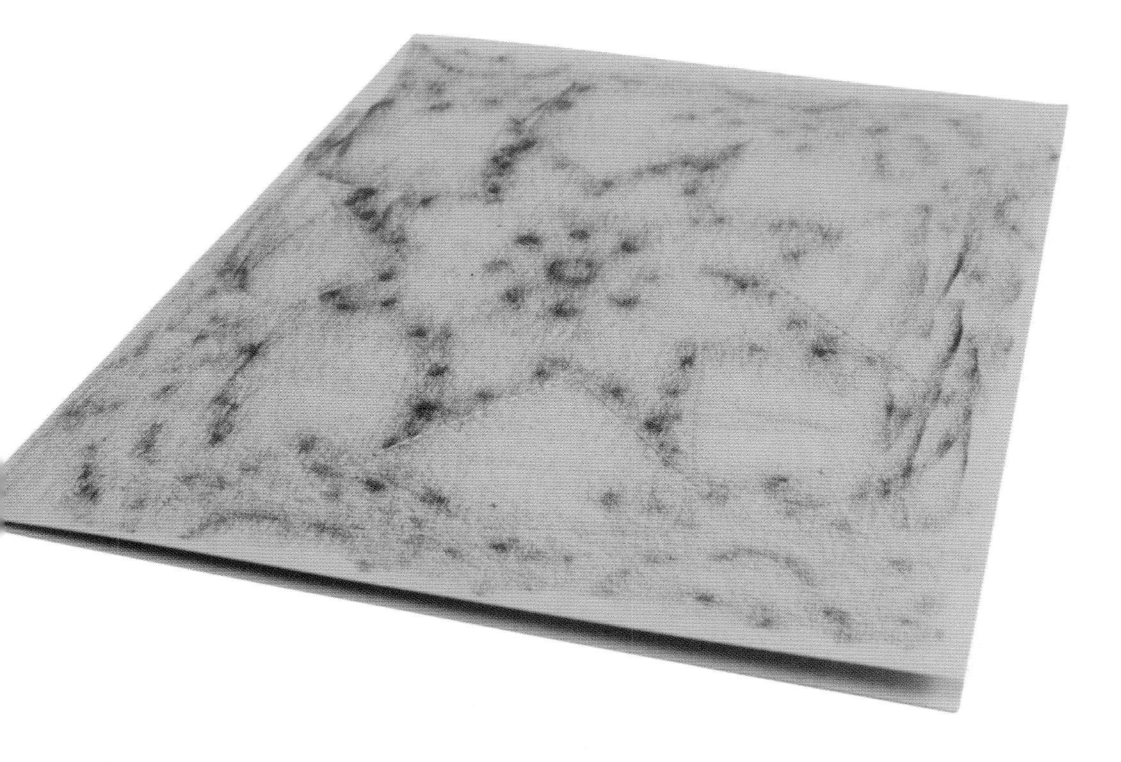

Your Name Here

Personalize cards while using the name as part of the design.

MATERIALS

- Square green card stock, folded
- Letter stencils
- 1 ultrafine black marker
- 1 pink Sharpie marker
- Pink thread, for sewing
- Green thread, for bobbin

INSTRUCTIONS

1. Hold the card open and flat, face up.
2. Choose a name to use for the card.
3. Keeping the letters in their correct order, divide them into two or three rows of three or four letters per row.
4. One at a time, position each stencil letter on the card. Trace with an ultrafine black marker.

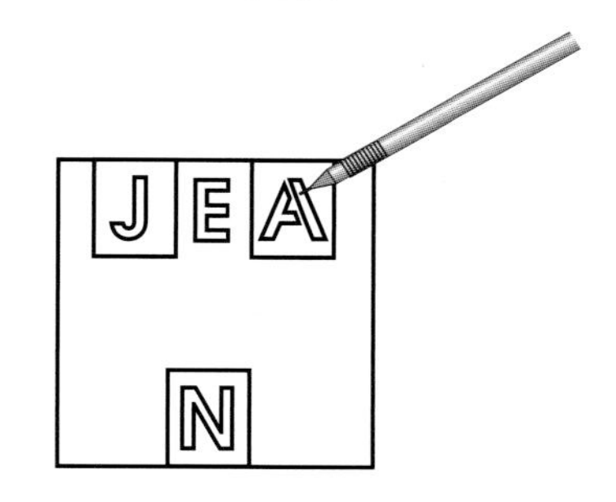

5. Fill in all letters with a pink Sharpie marker, and allow to dry.

6. Sew straight stitches near and between each of the letters, both horizontally and vertically.

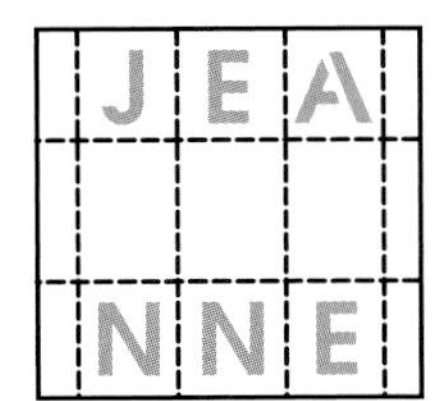

7. Trim the edges of any loose threads on the front and inside of the card.

Celebrating the New Year

Ring in a new year with cards to mark the new date.

MATERIALS

- Rectangular horizontal lilac card stock, folded
- Number stencils
- 1 ultrafine black marker
- 1 black Sharpie marker
- Various colors of thread, for sewing
- Lilac thread, for bobbin

INSTRUCTIONS

1. Hold the card open and flat, face up.
2. Position the first stencil number in the top left corner, and the fourth stencil number in the upper right corner of the card front. Trace with an ultrafine black marker.
3. Position stencil numbers two and three between the first and fourth numbers at the top, and trace.

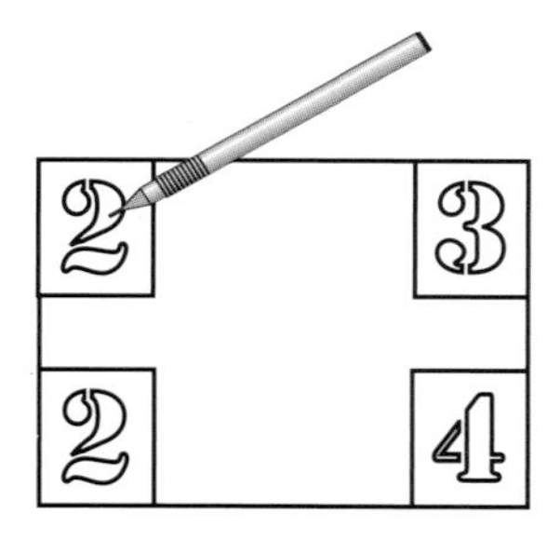

4. Position the first stencil number on the bottom left corner, and the fourth stencil number in the bottom right corner of the card front, and trace.

5. Position stencil numbers two and three between the first and fourth numbers at the bottom, and trace.

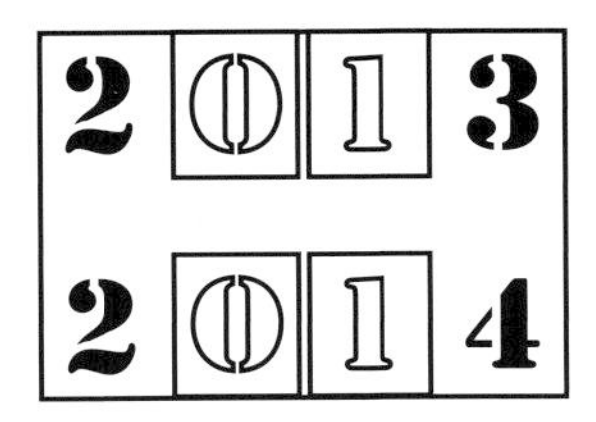

6. Fill in all numbers with a black Sharpie marker, and allow to dry.

7. Starting at the top of the card front, near the card fold, sew straight stitches over the top numbers, stopping at or near the bottom numbers, using many colors of brightly colored thread.

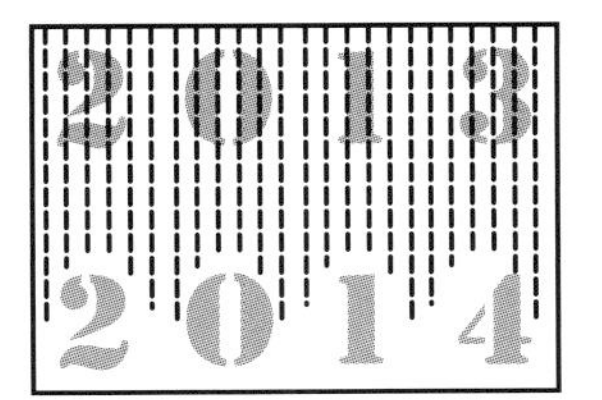

8. Trim the edges of any loose threads on the front and inside of the card.

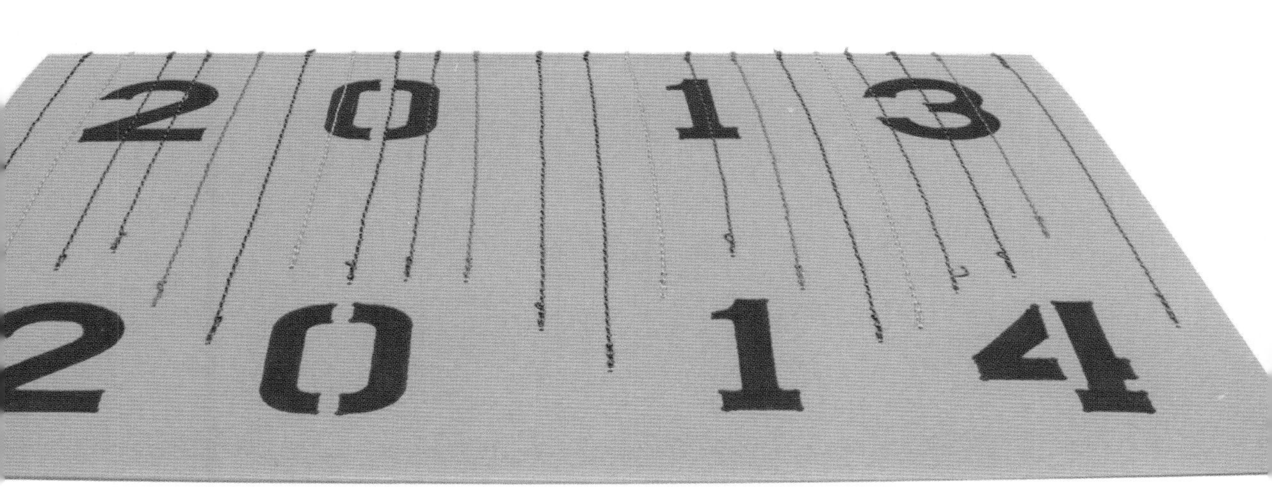

CHAPTER 5

Envelopes

When creating and sending your own cards, you're most likely going to want an envelope before you hand or mail it to the recipient. The store where you purchase card stock will likely also sell envelopes, either included with the card stock or available separately.

If envelopes are not available for the card stock, or if you used the card stock included in the back of this book, you may want to consider making your own envelopes.

This chapter includes instructions about how to make two different envelopes, depending on the size of the envelope paper relative to the card size. They are virtually the same envelope; the only difference between the two is the number of sides that require stitching. One is created by folding one large piece of paper, and then stitching three sides closed. The other requires two pieces of paper, and stitching all four sides of the envelope closed.

Creating your own envelopes may not only be a cost savings, or the solution to finding the correct size, but it also can offer the opportunity for you to decorate it so that it either coordinates with the art inside or makes it look unique, just as your card will be.

While the possibilities for decorating an envelope can be found with just about any card project included in this book, I suggest that you focus mainly on adapting the projects in the "Surface Design" chapter. If you decide to adapt a project from the "Fabric and Paper" or "Recycled Objects" chapter, make the design as flat as possible by stitching everything down more than you might on the card itself. It would be unfortunate if the art on your envelope were to get stuck on a sorting machine at the post office.

If you're going to be mailing a handmade envelope, pay attention to potential postage costs as you create it, as it may be a nonstandard size and/or require hand stamping by your postal clerk.

Simple One-Piece Stitched Envelope

Create a simple stitched envelope for stitched cards!

MATERIALS

- 1 (8 1/2 x 11-inch [21.5 x 28 cm]) sheet of off-white flat card stock
- 1 (5 x 7-inch [12.5 x 18 cm]) or smaller decorated card
- Ruler
- Pencil
- Black thread, for sewing and bobbin

INSTRUCTIONS

1. Hold the flat card stock in the portrait position.

2. Fold it in half so it is 5 1/2 x 8 1/2 inches (14 x 21.5 cm) when folded. Rub the folded edge with your fingernail, a bone folder, or a clean, hard object so it has a firm crease.

3. Place a decorated card on the folded card stock near the fold, to assess whether the envelope card stock needs to be trimmed smaller. Be sure to have a minimum of 1/2 inch (1.3 cm) all around the open edges. Remove the card and trim to a smaller size if needed.

4. Using the presser foot of the sewing machine as a guide, sew straight stitches near one of the shorter ends of the folded card stock. Repeat on the opposite side.

5. Place the decorated card inside the stitched envelope.

6. Using the presser foot as a guide, sew straight stitches near the top edge of the card stock to enclose the card inside the envelope.

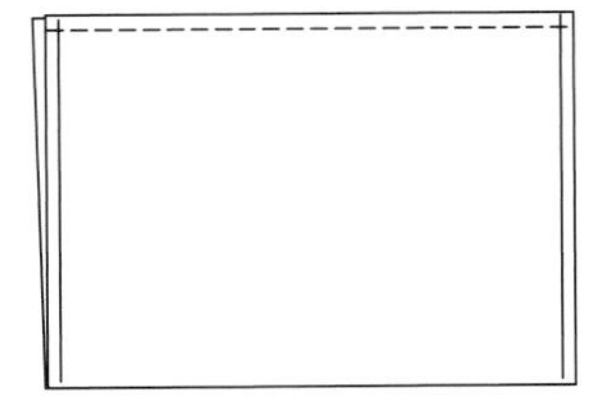

7. Trim the ends of any loose threads on the front and back sides of the envelope.

Simple One-Piece Stitched Envelope with Zigzag Edges

Sew zigzag stitches as additional decoration on an envelope.

MATERIALS

- 1 (8 1/2 x 11-inch [21.5 x 28 cm]) sheet of gray flat card stock
- 1 (5 x 7-inch [12.5 x 18 cm]) or smaller decorated card
- Ruler
- Pencil
- White thread, for sewing and bobbin

INSTRUCTIONS

1. Follow instructions 1 to 6 for the Simple One-Piece Stitched Envelope on page 131.

2. Sew zigzag stitches around the three edges of the envelope near the straight stitches.

3. Trim the ends of any loose threads on the front and back sides of the envelope.

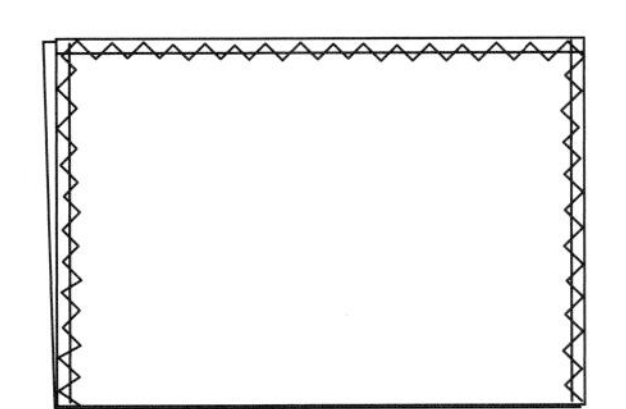

Stamped One-Piece Stitched Envelope

Stamp a design on a simple stitched envelope.

MATERIALS

- 1 (8 1/2 x 11-inch [21.5 x 28 cm]) sheet of white flat card stock
- 1 (5 x 7-inch [12.5 x 18 cm]) or smaller decorated card
- Ruler
- Pencil
- Heart-shaped eraser stamp (see page 14)
- Red inked stamp pad
- White thread, for sewing and bobbin

INSTRUCTIONS

1. Follow instructions 1 to 7 for the Simple One-Piece Stitched Envelope on page 131.

2. Press the heart-shaped eraser into the inked stamp pad. Press the inked heart stamp near one bottom corner of the envelope. Stamp the other bottom corner, and stamp in the bottom center. Repeat two more times, stamping between the corner hearts and the center stamp. Be sure to re-ink each time before you stamp. When you're finished, five hearts will be printed in a row at the bottom of the card stock. Refer to page 15 for technique suggestions.

3. Allow the ink to dry before proceeding according to the instructions on page 15.

Simple Two-Piece Stitched Envelope

Create a stitched envelope using two separate pieces of card stock.

MATERIALS

- 2 (8 1/2 x 11-inch [21.5 x 28 cm]) sheets of green flat card stock (or use different colors)
- 1 (7 1/2 x 7 1/2-inch [19 x 19 cm]) or smaller decorated card
- Ruler
- Pencil
- Blue thread, for sewing and bobbin (or use different colors for the top and bobbin)

INSTRUCTIONS

1. Hold the flat card stock in the portrait position.
2. Place a decorated card on the card stock to assess how much the paper needs to be trimmed. Be sure to leave a minimum of a 1/2-inch (1.3 cm) excess on all sides. Remove the card, and trim to the desired size.

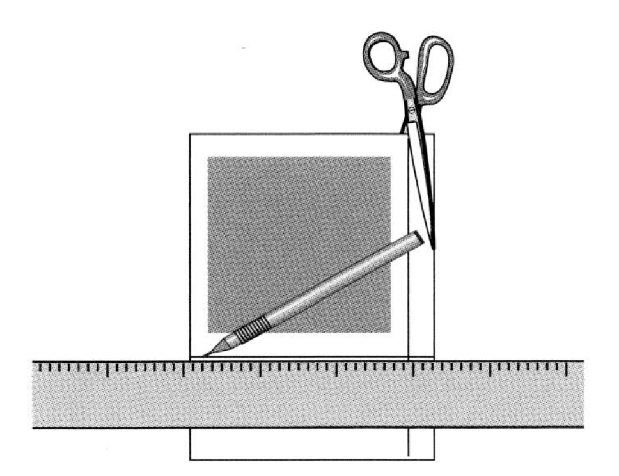

3. Trim the second piece of card stock to the same size.
4. Hold both pieces of trimmed card stock together. Using the presser foot of the sewing machine as a guide, sew straight stitches near one of the sides of the card stock. Repeat by stitching two more sides of the card stock.

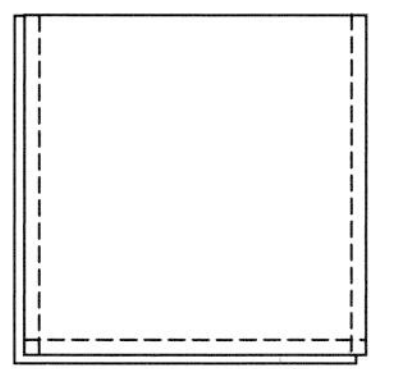

5. Place the decorated card inside the stitched envelope.
6. Using the presser foot as a guide, sew straight stitches near the top edge of the card stock, to enclose the card inside the envelope.

7. Trim the ends of any loose threads on the front and back sides of the envelope.

Stamped Two-Piece Stitched Envelope

Stitch and stamp a design on the front of an envelope.

MATERIALS

- 2 (8 1/2 x 11-inch [22 x 28 cm]) sheets of yellow flat card
- 1 (7 1/2 x 7 1/2-inch [19 x 19 cm]) or smaller decorated card
- Ruler
- Pencil
- 1 flower-shaped rubber eraser
- 1 pencil with unused eraser
- Red inked stamp pad
- White inked stamp pad
- Green thread, for sewing
- Yellow thread, for sewing and bobbin

INSTRUCTIONS

1. Follow instructions 1 to 3 for the Simple Two-Piece Stitched Envelope on page 136.

2. Using green thread, sew a straight stitch to sew a stem and two leaves at the bottom right side of one piece of envelope card stock, being careful to keep the stitching at least 1/2 inch (1.3 cm) away from the outer edge.

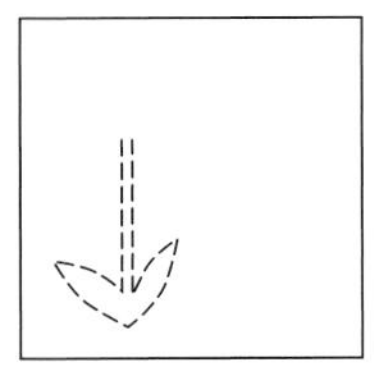

3. Trim the ends of loose threads on the front and back sides of the card stock.

4. Press the flower shape eraser into the red inked stamp pad. Press the inked stamp on the card stock at the top of the stitched stem. Refer to page 15 for technique suggestions. Allow the ink to dry before proceeding.

5. Using the unused eraser end of a pencil, press it into the white inked stamp pad and stamp the eraser in the middle of the flower design. Allow the ink to dry before proceeding.

6. Follow instructions 4 to 7 for the Simple Two-Piece Stitched Envelope on page 136, using yellow thread when sewing.

Resources

While you may already have many of the materials you need to make your cards, here is a resource list with suggestions to help you find what you don't already have. Most items can be found in many more locations than those mentioned below, but these vendors are easily accessible to different parts of the United States.

THE PAPER SOURCE (www.paper-source.com or 1-888-PAPER-11): folded cards—square (5 1/2 x 5 1/2 inch [14 x 14 cm]), A7 (5 x 7 inch [12.5 x 18 cm])

MICHAELS (www.michaels.com or 1-800-642-4235): card stock and envelopes, unfolded card stock, and Recollections Cardstock Essentials 3 x 6 inch (7.5 x 15 cm), sold in 100-sheet packages; decorative leaves

JOANN FABRICS AND CRAFTS (www.joann.com or 1-888-739-4120): fabric, zippers, yarn, lace, ribbon, rickrack, and string

AMAZON.COM: Strathmore postcards 4 x 6-inch (10 x 15 cm) pad of 15, Color Box Pigment Stamp Pads (acid free), patterned stamps, sushi grass, 35 mm clear slide pages, Stencils-HY-KO 1 in. Letters, Numbers and Symbols Stencil Set, and Fiskars Paper Edgers

WAWAK (www.wawak.com or 1-800-654-2235): scissors, sewing needles, and thread

STAPLES (www.staples.com or 1-800-STAPLES): X-Acto Light Utility Knife #2 with #11, Sharpie permanent markers, plastic name tag holder, glue, large or antiroll crayons, colored pencils, pencils, rulers, shaped children's rubber erasers

JERRY'S ARTARAMA (www.jerrysartarama.com or 1-800-U-ARTIST): Able-Rub or other art gum rubber erasers (1 x 1 x 1 inch [2.5 x 2.5 x 2.5 cm])

LOWES (www.lowes.com) or HOME DEPOT (www.homedepot.com or 1-800-HOME-DEPOT): orange construction fencing

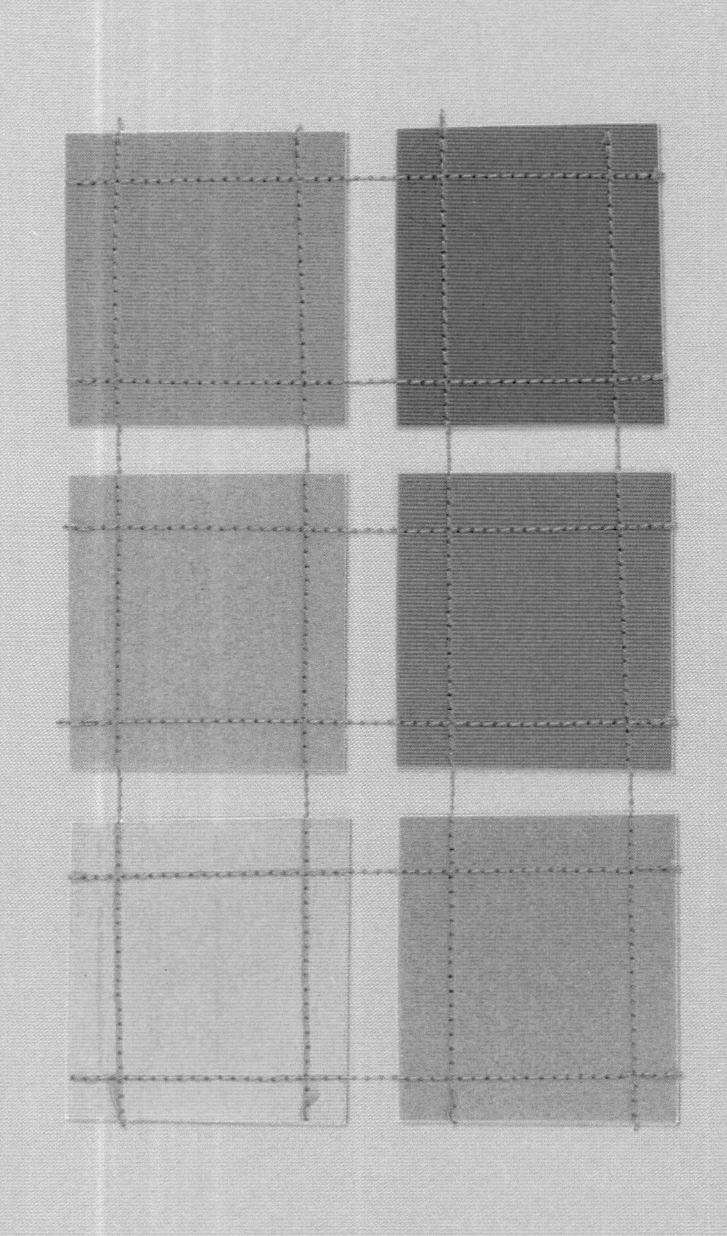

Index